The Lottery Book

The Lottery Book

The Truth Behind the Numbers

Don Catlin

**Foreword by
Frank Scoblete**

Chicago and Los Angeles

07   06   05   04   03   5   4   3   2   1

Library of Congress Cataloging-in-Publication Data

Catlin, Don.
   The lottery book : the truth behind the numbers / Don Catlin ; foreword by Frank Scoblete.
       p. cm.
Includes bibliographical references and index.
   ISBN 1-56625-193-1
   1. Lotteries—United States. 2. Gambling—United States. I. Title.

   HG6126.C38 2003
   795.3'8'0973—dc21

                                        2003004233

Bonus Books
875 N. Michigan Ave., Ste. 1416
Chicago, IL 60611

Printed in the United States of America

This book is dedicated to my family:
Mary, Jeffrey, Jennifer,
Andrea, Larry, Scott, Tyler,
Nathaniel, and Jacob.

Table of Contents

Foreword
by Frank Scoblete

A few years ago, I won $1,600 in the New York State Lotto, and I was miserable for two days. Here's why:

I live in a little village with a population of nine thousand souls just outside New York City on Long Island (we always say *on* Long Island, not *in* Long Island). Although we comprise a goodly cross-section of New York occupations—teachers, doctors, lawyers, firefighters, police, businessmen and women, and one gambling writer—the town itself is a throwback to another time.

My little village has no shopping malls, no fast-food joints, no industry, and little crime. Almost everyone knows everyone else—or, at least, everyone knows someone who knows just about everyone else. We have a five-block "main street" where you'll find: restaurants, a liquor store, a couple of banks, a bar, several beauty salons, two delicatessens, some law offices, three stationery stores, and a small train station. We have a movie theater that shows "independent" films, that is, films you are not ever likely to see at the vast multiplexes that litter the rest of the Long Island landscape. We have our own police department, our own volunteer fire department, our own volunteer ambulance corps, and our own department of public works. I live in the real Pleasantville, and it's in living color to boot.

The people in my little village are very active. There are clubs and organizations of every kind, sports teams, Christmas and Hanukkah festivals, country fairs, trips to "the city" (that means Manhattan), and, oh, yes, one other thing . . .

Gambling.

Especially on lottery tickets.

Most especially on lottery tickets.

The three stationery stores and the liquor store sell scratch-offs and chances to win New York State's Lotto for millions, and to win the multistate Mega Millions for even more millions. In the morning when I buy my papers, there are always three or four people queued up at any one of the three stationery stores with a list of the numbers they're going to play. Commuters heading for work in the city stop by to grab a cup of coffee, buy a scratch-off, get a "quick pick" for the big drawing, then scoot out the door when they hear the train whistle blowing. Later in the day, you'll see many of the retired folks walking down the main street, scratching off lottery tickets or holding their picks for the Lotto or Mega Millions jackpots. Some people play every day, and I've come to know them.

There's the disheveled chain-smoking woman who spends at least $20 a day on the daily numbers, on her carefully thought-out picks for the various mega-jackpots, and on a handful of scratch-offs. Between hacks, coughs, and wheezes, she'll rattle off her numbers and her philosophy of gambling: "I gotta win someday. I'm due. This is the lucky store."

She's right about that last statement. The stationery store where she buys her tickets *is* lucky, if by "lucky" we mean it has sold a $25 million winning ticket and several hundred-thousand-dollar prizes. Of the four lottery stores in the five blocks of my little village, it gets the most play—and, since it does, it also tends to have the most winners. This is dutifully noted on the front window and on every available wall space in the store. Even my $1,600 prize is up on the wall, in a corner, near the newspaper stand. The paper on which my great good fortune is immortalized is yellow with age and looking increasingly more brittle; I guess that's because my achievement hangs near the door. But, then, I'm only a minor winner in the great lottery scheme of things, and I guess I don't deserve one of the hallowed places near the cash register and quick-pick machine where everyone can gaze, and dream of telling their bosses, "Go fly a kite, I'm rich! I don't need your job anymore!"

The owner of the store is a pleasant fellow from India named Anail Singh. Everyone calls him "Bill." That's because he got sick of people calling him "a nail" when it's pronounced "a nile," ("as in the river," he'd say) until he finally gave up and said, "Actually, call me Bill." So everyone now calls him Bill.

Bill says, "Everybody love the lottery. The bigger the prize the better."

Most of the people in my little village who play the lotteries or the scratch-off tickets are acutely unaware of the odds that they face. Tommy, a 68-year-old retired bartender at a local pub, now a "kinda gardener," doesn't let odds scare him: "You think I don't know it's millions to one against? Of course, I know."

I told him it's about 13-million-to-one against on the

Lotto and about 135-million-to-one against on the Mega Millions.

"Yeah? Well, those numbers mean nothing. Someone's gotta win, right?" Indeed, ultimately someone does win, no doubt about it. But what are the real chances that the someone will be you?

Lillie, a "60-something" grandmother who doesn't look a day over 50 ("Make sure you write I don't look a day over 50"), plays $10 a week. "I play three dollars on the Tuesday drawing, three dollars on the Friday drawing, and three dollars on the Saturday drawing, then I buy one scratch-off on Sunday. I've won several times but nothing more than one hundred dollars. I don't really think I'll win; I just do it to dream."

Dan, the dashing commuter, plays because "it's a way out of working for the next 30 years of my life. At least there's hope." Another guy, Steve, who buys his lottery tickets at the liquor store says, "Gambling is much more fun than drinking. I gave up drinking, mostly gave it up except for wine with dinner, but I'd never give up the lottery. I buy about a dozen tickets a week. I can afford it."

When the jackpots rise, as Bill says, the action at all four lottery outlets gets hot and heavy. Even the liquor store does a brisk business during such times. And it was during one of those big-jackpot weeks, when the New York Lotto was above $40 million, that I played. I'm one of the people that Don Catlin, the author of the book you're holding, chides for trying to make a case for a "good" lottery bet. At $40 million dollars, the New York Lotto becomes a "good" game in the sense that the winner will get more money back than the odds he or she faces. The Lotto I played was about a 13-million-to-one shot. If the winner got the whole $40 million, he could expect to gross $20 million (if he chose "lump sum," which I did), and, after the government taxed his $20 million, he could expect to clear about $15 million. So, I faced a 13-million-to-one shot, but if I won I'd get $15 million or so. Not bad.

So when Lotto gets to $40 million, I play, and when Mega Millions gets to $135 million, I play. I'll buy five dollars worth of tickets and play each game until someone wins. Then I'll wait for the lotteries to get to my pre-established totals again. As silly as this sounds, I feel as if I'm making a good wager by doing this.

So that fateful Wednesday, I bought Lotto tickets for that night's drawing. The next morning I took my usual walk around town and got my papers at Bill's store. I didn't even inquire about the Lotto because, frankly, I had forgotten about it. I was busy thinking about some article I was writing.

At breakfast, I remembered that I had bought a ticket, so I took it out of my wallet, opened the *New York Post* to page 2 and checked out the numbers. I had the first number; I had the second number; I had the third number *(Is it possible that I could win this thing?)*; I had the fourth number *(I think four numbers wins some money. God! Is that my heart? My heart is beating like crazy. There's an outside chance I could win this thing!)*; I had the fifth number! *(Oh, my, God, where is the sixth number? I'm gonna win this thing! It's at the top of the page. Just go to the top of the page and find out if you have that sixth number and then you'll sell your small ranch home; buy a home in Las Vegas, a home on the North Fork of Long Island; a home in . . . wherever. Then you'll give your sons and parents . . . however much and . . . where is that damn number? God, I'll be rich! Oh, my heart . . .).* I didn't have the sixth number. I was one number away, one stinking number.

It wasn't until the next day that I realized that the five numbers I had would be a decent win. In my disappointment, I had forgotten all about the "little wins" because that big monster had been staring me in the face. I called the Lotto office on Friday and asked what I had won. "You matched five numbers, you win $1,600." It did take me a few days to get rid of the disappointment. I tried to console myself by thinking that at least this $1,600 would almost assure me of being ahead of the Lotto when I died (for a gambler, being ahead when you snuff it is the ultimate goal). I figured that, based on my play, I'd spend about $60 a year on lottery tickets. It would take me 26.6 years of *losing every single ticket I ever bought* for me to lose back that $1,600.

Since then I *have* lost on every single ticket I've bought. I haven't won a single dollar. When those jackpots get into the stratosphere I still feel that adrenaline flowing. I join the chain-smoking lady, Tommy the "kinda gardener," Dan the commuter, Lillie "who doesn't look a day over 50," and Steve, who now drinks wine with dinner, in dreaming those millionaire dreams when buying tickets from Bill.

The book you're holding in your hands should be read by every American who plays the state-run lotteries. Despite the fact that we players all know "the odds are millions-to-one against" winning those big jackpots, most of us don't know the nature of these games or the math behind them.

We don't know how to increase our chances of winning a jackpot that doesn't have to be shared with other players; which numbers to pick to achieve such an end; and how to keep the long and greedy arm of the government from getting its hands on significant portions of such a win. This book will explain how to protect yourself should you win.

The author of *The Lottery Book,* Don Catlin, professor emeritus at the University of Massachusetts, knows his way around the numbers game. Catlin has worked for the government designing submarine guidance systems; he's been a consultant to the casino industry concerning game design and results, and, most important (to me), he's one of the mainstays of my Web site, *www.scoblete.com.* In short, the guy knows gambling inside and out, and he knows the underlying math behind all the games we gambling-lovers love to play. But, unlike many mathematicians who analyze gambling, Catlin is not an ivory-tower pundit steeped only in theory like a wine "expert" who only knows the chemical composition of a vintage, not its taste and bouquet and the warm glow it gives as it goes down. No, sir, Don Catlin is also a player. He knows the thrills involved in challenging chance.

The Lottery Book is a roadmap to state-run lotteries all over the country. It's a trip into the how and why of both jackpot lotteries and scratch-off tickets. While there's one chapter that's heavy on the math for those of you who, like me, are not mathletes, it is still a book that is accessible to all of us. And don't shy away from understanding the math; with a small effort, you'll achieve a good grasp of the way these games are structured. Catlin will take you step-by-step through the process of analyzing the games; no rush, take your time and enjoy the lessons.

But *The Lottery Book* is not a pedantic exercise in analysis. Far from it. You'll meet people who have captured lottery lightning in a bottle; people who have won the dream-those-impossible-dreams jackpots. Some winners have gotten to live the dream to its fullest; some others saw the dream turn into a nightmare.

And do you know just how far back lotteries go in history? And how many cultures actually used them to finance wars, luxuries, and religion? You'll find those fascinating facts in this book as well.

Enjoy.

Now, do you really think I can go a whole 26.6 years without winning *anything?*

Acknowledgments

I would like to express my sincere thanks to Frank Scoblete for his help in writing this book. Not only did Frank read the entire manuscript, making many corrections and helpful suggestions, but it was also he who encouraged me to take on the project in the first place. I'm glad that he did, for it turned out to be a fascinating study that was more interesting than I had expected. Thank you, Frank. Thanks too to the many lotteries that responded to my requests for information, 35 in all. Special thanks to Bret Toyne from the Multistate Lottery Corporation for answering my repeated requests. Also a warm thank you to Beth Burgess of the Kentucky Lottery, who not only wished me well on my book but also gave me a good lead on a very useful Web site. My friend and colleague Dave Foulis read the manuscript and made some helpful suggestions; my thanks to him. A hearty "thank you" to Maxine Nelson, whose inquiry to me is responsible for the section on anonymity in Chapter 5. Copyeditor Caroline Greeven and managing editor Devon Freeny of Bonus Books each read my manuscript with great care and made many, many improvements; I sincerely appreciate all of their hard work. Last, but certainly not least, thanks to my wife Mary. Mary not only read each chapter as I finished it, making corrections and suggestions, but also tolerated my occasional bouts of frustration and disappointment with her usual patience and good humor.

1

California Dreamin'

Primm

Driving east from Los Angeles toward Las Vegas on June 18, 2001, the subject of state lotteries is the farthest thing from my mind. It is a sunny and warm Monday morning, and my wife Mary and I have decided to take the scenic route through the San Gabriel Mountains. We are on Route 2, the primary east-west route through the beautifully cool and verdant hills. The scenery is spectacular: the mountain vistas surround us, punctuating our trip with peaks of four and five thousand feet. The "real world" seems far away, though I'd have to admit that as we head toward Las Vegas thoughts of gambling are rolling around in the recesses of my brain. State lotteries though? No, that mental leap hasn't happened yet. Little do I realize, however, that before this trip has ended, the connection will happen, big time.

California is a state of contrasts, home to scrubby desert plants in the southwest and magnificent redwood trees in the northern coastal regions. A drive west along Sunset Boulevard takes you from the fast food joints, nightclubs, and dive bars of Hollywood to the most elegant, sculptured, and glamorous residential area in LA: Beverly Hills (home to the only post office in the United States with valet parking).

The lowest place in the nation is in Death Valley at a spot called Badwater, 282 feet below sea level. From here you can see the peak of Mount Whitney, which at 14,495 feet is the highest spot in the lower 48. For Mary and me, a similarly dramatic contrast awaits us as we near the end of Route 2. Here the final view is one not of green mountains and valleys but of a flat, brown desert unfolding before our windshield. The change from the mountains is impressive. We make our way down from the mountains toward Cajon Junction to pick up I-15, the highway that leads to Las Vegas. At Cajon Junction there is a grass fire, and firemen from surrounding towns have teamed up to battle the blaze, which is burning out of control in the parched desert scrub. Our ramp is closed and we have to backtrack before we finally get on I-15.

Once on I-15 we head toward hot and windy Barstow, our lunch and gas stop, and the last city of any size before we arrive in Las Vegas. We eat quickly and are happy to continue on our way. Driving on, we pass the town of Baker, the California entryway to Death Valley, and read what is advertised as the world's tallest thermometer. It says 112 degrees.

On we go through the high desert country, cruising

through interchanges that lead to nowhere, and whipping past signs to strange destinations like "Zzyzzx Road". Finally, in the distance, we see Primm, a Nevada town that lies right on the border with California. "Town" might be an overstatement: Primm comprises three casino hotels and three gas stations, two golf courses, an RV park, and one hell of a big roller coaster. There's no post office and no grocery store, but naturally there's an outlet shopping mall. We're heading for Buffalo Bill's, one of the two casinos on the east side of I-15, when we witness a strange phenomenon, and it's one of the most bizarre sights I've ever seen. In the unbearable heat of a Nevada June, hundreds of people are standing in a long, slowly moving line that makes its way into a small building on the California side of the border. Weird!

A couple of questions to casino personnel clears up the mystery. About a hundred feet over the California-Nevada border is a California Lottery outlet known as the Primm Valley Lotto Store. Though I did later notice that there is a sign near the store, I hadn't seen it at that point, and I didn't know the store existed. The line of people we saw were waiting to buy California State Lottery tickets, specifically tickets for the California Super Lotto Plus game. The drawing for this game, held on June 23, would have a big prize estimated to be in the $140 million range, however, the chance of winning it, as we will later see, would be minuscule. Nevertheless, that is a lot of money, and winning it might change one's life. I can see the headline: "Massachusetts Tourist Wins California Dream." On the other hand, it sure is hot outside.

Curiouser and Curiouser

We leave Primm (with no lottery tickets) and settle in at the Rio in Las Vegas. I snap on the TV for local news and sure enough there is a segment on Primm and the lottery. The Super Lotto Plus jackpot is the largest in California history and, for this reason, is getting an unusually large play. I learn that the people melting in the desert sun in Primm are waiting an average of three hours to get their tickets. These people are certainly not from California. I doubt if many of them are from Arizona, as Arizona has its own lottery. The bulk of them have to be from Las Vegas, 41 miles to the north. These folks have driven 41 miles or more, from a city that offers some of the most exciting gambling in the world, to stand out in the desert sun for three hours just to buy lottery tickets. I am intrigued. I dig deeper.

In the early part of the twentieth century the area know today as Primm Valley was simply called State Line. The only road through the area in those days was Route 91 and it was not all that great. Part of the land in the area was owned by a cantankerous old coot by the name of Pete McIntyre, a former miner. Pete ran a ramshackle Mobil gas station known as Whiskey Pete's, the only structure in the area. There was not a lot of traffic in those days (remember, gambling was not legalized in Nevada until 1931), so most of Pete's money came from bootlegging, which explains the gas station's moniker.

Pete died of miner's lung in 1933, and the land and gas station changed hands a few times after his death. In the 1950s the Reno entrepreneur Ernest Primm, owner of the

Reno-based Primadonna Corporation, and a contemporary and competitor of Reno casino mogul William F. Harrah, bought the Mobil gas station and land. He also bought eight hundred surrounding acres owned by the federal government, some of which was in California, and filed water rights with the Bureau of Land Management. To satisfy the bureau's requirements for ownership, Primm planted barley fields and tended them for three years. When the required time was up he plowed them under and began expanding the Mobil station. He also added a saloon with a few slot machines and a 12-room motel; as time passed the motel grew and more slots were added as well.

Ernest Primm died in 1981 at the age of 73, and his son Gary took over the Primadonna Corporation and kept building. In 1994 Buffalo Bill's opened in State Line. Whiskey Pete's and Primm Valley Resort soon followed. In 1996, following a suggestion from a Las Vegas reporter, State Line was renamed Primm in honor of its founder Ernest Primm. This renaming also solved a bit of confusion in that State Line was not an official designation and was in conflict with Stateline, Nevada, which was an officially named town near Reno. In 1997, the first Primadonna Corporation golf course opened in Primm. On January 3 of the same year, Primadonna Corporation opened New York, New York casino and hotel on the northwest corner of Las Vegas and Tropicana Boulevards, a site owned by MGM Grand Corporation.

In the '90s Gary Primm negotiated with the state of California and opened the Dry Lakes Lottery Store in California on land he himself—and not Primadonna Corporation—owned. In 1999, the MGM Grand bought Primadonna

Resorts, Inc., taking 100 percent ownership of New York, New York and all of the Primadonna properties in Primm, Nevada. Later in the year 2000, MGM Grand bought out Mirage Resorts, forming the MGM-Mirage Corporation. Finally, on May 3, 2001, a month or so before my stop there, a subsidiary of MGM-Mirage known as Primm Valley Resorts bought the Dry Lakes Lotto Store from Gary Primm for an undisclosed price and changed its name to the Primm Valley Lotto Store. Had I ventured a guess at the sale price on that hot day in June I'm sure that whatever figure I named would have been much too low. Why? Here are the startling facts.

During the year 2000, the Dry Lakes Lotto Store was the state of California's leading lottery outlet, with $6.2 million in ticket sales. The closest competitor was a Los Angeles liquor store with $1.2 million in sales. These figures become more significant when you consider the population densities of California and Nevada, and they help to explain the phenomenal growth in state lotteries that we will explore in the next chapter.

Oh, yeah, did the "California Dreamin'" become a reality for anyone? On June 23 the winning numbers for the California Super Lotto Plus were drawn; the big prize, as predicted, was $141 million. On June 29, a 66-year-old retired grocery clerk named Alcairo Castellano, a resident of San Jose, brought the winning ticket to the lottery's San Francisco district office. He chose to take the money in a lump sum, which meant that he received $70,794,364, or about $42.3 million after taxes. At the time this jackpot was the largest single-state jackpot in U.S. lottery history. The largest previous single-state lottery prize was $118.8 million in 1991, also in California.

Castellano told the *San Jose Mercury News* that he had bought his ticket on Saturday at a local liquor store and let the machine pick the numbers. On Sunday when he awoke, Mr. Castellano made coffee, plucked his ticket from the refrigerator where he had placed it, opened his paper and began matching the numbers one by one. "Now, what's going on here?" he said to himself. "Is this real? I can't believe it!" As it turned out, two weeks earlier the couple had been thinking of selling their house and moving south. Instead they stayed, enjoying their three grandchildren and participating in community service.

Mr. Castellano was the only winner, so all those folks who traveled to Primm would have to try their luck again.

2

The Numbers Game Becomes Legit

Live Free or Die

The people of New Hampshire are an independent sort, and their state motto "Live Free or Die" is taken so seriously that it is printed on every state license plate. The phrase "live free" is especially poignant for a Massachusetts resident; Massachusetts currently has a 5 percent sales tax plus a state income tax, while there is no state sales tax in New Hampshire. As a result, New Hampshire businesses in border towns such as Nashua flourish with customers from Massachusetts. A friend who lives in Nashua puts it this way: "If Massachusetts didn't exist we would have to invent it." New Hampshire's state-owned liquor stores also sell large quantities of liquor to folks from Massachusetts. Lest you think that marketing liquor to the residents of Massachusetts is unintentional, a drive north on I-93 out of Boston will soon disabuse you of any such notion. As soon as you cross the New Hampshire State line the road widens and within a mile of the line, conveniently situated on the median, is a State of New Hampshire liquor store.

Although I'm no mind reader, I suspect that back in 1953, when State Representative Larry Pickett from Keene, New Hampshire, first proposed a sweepstakes bill, he had visions of Bay Staters streaming over the border to gamble in New Hampshire. Pickett's pitch was that the Sweepstakes would be a voluntary, and profitable, method of raising revenue for education. He lobbied and gained support for his bill and on April 30, 1963, governor John King finally signed the sweepstakes bill into law. The first three-member Sweepstakes Commission was sworn into office on August 1, 1963. Local Option voting was held on March 10, 1964, by special ballot. This allowed the cities and towns in New Hampshire to vote for or against the sale of sweepstakes tickets in their community. Only 13 of the state's 211 communities voted disapproval of the measure and on March 12, 1964, Sweepstakes tickets went on sale.

The original New Hampshire Sweepstakes was patterned after the Irish Hospital's Sweepstakes. It combined a lottery with horse races at New Hampshire's Rockingham Park. The name "Sweepstakes," and the tie to horse races was designed to avoid the 70-year-old federal anti-lottery statutes (more on this later). There were two Sweepstakes drawings a year, one in July and one in September, with small monthly drawings designed to keep up interest during the long stretches between the large drawings. The tickets were three dollars each. Players wrote their names on the tickets, and the commission stored these until drawings were held in conjunction with two specific races at Rockingham. The details are unimportant, as this form of the lottery has long since ceased, and new games with larger prizes and better revenue potential have taken its place. The original Sweepstakes game was not as successful as some had hoped, but neither did it fold as some had predicted, and as changes were instituted it eventually become a huge success. More importantly, this first game was also the catalyst that began the lottery fever that swept the United States during the rest of the century.

Did the residents of Massachusetts play the New Hampshire Lottery? Remember the Primm Valley Lotto Store? It took Massachusetts 10 years to finally stem the outflow of revenue and create its own lottery. Nonetheless, we now spend much of our gambling money in the two Indian casinos in Connecticut; and, as for our liquor, well, we still buy it from New Hampshire.

Lotteries Before New Hampshire

Lotteries date back to 200 B.C. when the original version of Keno, somewhat different from its present form, was created during the Han Dynasty in China. The proceeds of the game were used primarily to construct the Great Wall of China. (We'll look at Keno in more detail later.) One of the first recorded European lotteries was held by the widow of the Flemish painter Jan Van Eyck in 1446, to dispose of his remaining paintings. The first municipal lottery to offer money as a prize was in Florence, Italy, and was called *La Lotto de Firenze*. It was so successful that other Italian cities followed, and the word *lottery* is believed to come from the Italian word *lotto*, which means "destiny" or "fate." In 1539, King Francis I of France authorized a lottery to replenish a shrinking treasury. Oddly enough, the treasury had been shrinking because funds from it had been flowing to foreign lotteries.

In 1567, Queen Elizabeth I established the first English state lottery; one delightfully suspicious lottery story involves her successor, King James I of England. In 1612, by royal decree, King James created a lottery whose proceeds were used to aid the first British colony in America. Here is the suspicious part: the Church of England held two of the three winning tickets for the first draw.

Other lottery events in Europe include the formation, in the Netherlands, of the oldest lottery still in operation (1726); the creation of a lottery in England in 1753 to establish the British Museum; the formation in 1776 of the *Loterie Royale* of the Military School (later Saint-Cyr) by Louis XV of France. This last lottery has historical significance because after its adoption other lotteries were outlawed, giving it the status of a monopoly within France. Eventually, this lottery became the French *Loterie Nationale*. These early European lotteries had little effect on America. In 1930, however, the Irish Hospital Sweepstakes was launched and because of the prohibition of lotteries in the U.S. and Canada (discussed below) this lottery had a large American market; again, the Primm Valley phenomenon in action.

Lotteries in the United States began in the 1700s; many were sponsored (and played) by our Founding Fathers. Benjamin Franklin used lotteries to finance cannons for the Revolutionary War; John Hancock ran a lottery whose proceeds were used to rebuild Faneuil Hall in Boston; and George Washington helped open westward expansion from Virginia by the construction of Mountain Road, a project funded by his lottery for the purpose. Thomas Jefferson, who was $80,000 in debt at the end of his life, used a lottery to dispose of most of his remaining property. After 1790, 24 of the 33 states ran lotteries to fund various civic improvements. During this period there were private lotteries as well, many of which funded churches and schools. It may surprise you that universities such as Harvard, Yale, Princeton, and Columbia were funded by such lotteries.

Lotteries were well established in the American psyche by 1868, when the Louisiana Lottery Company opened for business, and eventually grew to become the largest lottery in the country. Tickets were sold nationwide, and sales agents operated in every state in the union. Even though it appeared to be a state lottery, it was not; in fact, the lottery was privately owned. The State of Louisiana allowed the lottery to operate in exchange for a relatively small donation of $40,000 a year for 25 years to the Charity Hospital of New Orleans. The Louisiana Lottery Company kept the rest of the revenues, tax free, and earned millions of dollars. During this 25-year period some state legislatures reacted to this outflow of state cash by passing bans on lotteries operating in their state. The real crusher for this lottery, however, came in 1890, when Congress passed a law banning all lottery materials from the U.S. mail system. Probably because of this law, the 1894 Louisiana Legislature refused to extend the Lottery Company's charter, and the company disbanded its Louisiana operations and moved to Honduras.

When the details of the lottery's cushy arrangement with the state were made public, there were charges of bribery and scandal in (and by) the legislature, and questions were asked about why it had taken 25 years for this information to be made public. Finally, in 1895, Federal Congress passed a law banning all lottery materials from interstate commerce, and in 1905 the U.S. Supreme Court reaffirmed the states' use of police powers in controlling gambling. These laws, and the fact that lotteries were by then prohibited in most states by constitutional provisions, meant that no state was directly involved in a lottery or other gambling operation for the next 60 or so years. These provisions explain why the first lottery in New Hampshire was called a Sweepstakes and was tied to the legal activity of horse racing.

Interestingly, in 1924 the Puerto Rican legislature voted to create (actually recreate) a lottery. The U.S. Congress could have overridden this legislation, but it chose not to; and the Puerto Rican lottery is still in operation today. I believe its existence had little effect on gambling in the continental United States, so I will leave it at that.

What did have an effect on the continental United States, and was eventually affected by the creation of state lotteries, was an illegal lottery known as the Numbers Racket. The Numbers Racket was a spinoff of an earlier illegal lottery called Treasury Tickets. This was a lottery that operated during the 1920s, and it was called Treasury Tickets because the winning number was the last five numbers in the daily United States Treasury balance. Tickets cost 25¢, 35¢, 50¢, or one dollar. In an attempt to capture a larger market, some operators in New York's Harlem began to offer a 10¢ ticket. The 10¢ tickets were very popular, but unfortunately the cost of printing the tickets outweighed the profits.

Various operators tried other inexpensive alternatives, but the one that clicked was a lottery called Clearinghouse Numbers, which began in 1923. Players simply picked a three-digit number such as 579 and wrote it on a slip of unmarked paper. The winning number was the last three digits of the Cincinnati Clearinghouse daily balance, hence the name Clearinghouse Numbers. The winning payoff was at 499 to 1. The lottery was simple and honest (though clearly not fair), and its popularity soon spread beyond the Harlem community. The name evolved into simply the Numbers game.

In 1933, Prohibition in the United States ended and the country's bootleggers were out of business. Looking for a new racket, many of these hoodlums muscled in on existing Numbers operations and took over the operations by either killing or otherwise discouraging those operators who objected. By 1935 the Numbers game was run by the mob and it was known as the Numbers Racket. The Numbers, as run by the mob, maintained its popularity and eventually replaced Treasury Tickets.

I am sorry to say that I became a small cog in this form of organized crime during the summer of 1954. I had landed a job working at a filling station on one of the main routes through my hometown of Erie, Pennsylvania. I got the job because I already had some experience pumping gas and lubricating automobiles; unbeknownst to me, however, there were three other job requirements. First, I had to learn how to grease dump trucks. (This is easy enough as long as you remember to lower the load bed before you pull the truck out of the garage.) Second, I had to learn to change truck tires using only an adz mallet and tire irons. The third thing I had to learn was how to write numbers, as the service station was also a numbers drop (outlet). Of the three this was the easiest to learn but, of course, it was also illegal. To be honest with you, it didn't seem so bad at the time, but in retrospect I have to admit that the profits weren't going for bridges and schools. One of the good things I can say about state lotteries is that they did put the mob out of the numbers game.

My recollection is that most of the Numbers players we had were old ladies who phoned in their bets on a daily basis. (Today I probably wouldn't use the adjective "old" but at the time I was 18 years old and I thought anyone over 50 had one foot in the grave.) The operation was pretty much the same as that described above, except that the payoff then was 599 to 1. The player picked three digits—say, 579—and could bet as little as 25¢ on them occurring in the order 579. My recollection is that the winning numbers in those days depended on certain horse races.

A player could also "box" a number, which meant writing down the number and drawing a box around it, such as 579. This meant that you were also betting on the other five permutations of the number, that is, 597, 759, 795, 957, and 975. A typical bet would be $1 on the number and $1.25 on the box. This meant that your wager was $1 on the number 579 coming in (a return of $600) and 25¢ on each of the

permutations (a return of $150). It doesn't take much figur-
ing to see that, in the long run, the player was losing 40¢ on
the dollar (which we will later describe as a 40 percent
house edge). Naturally, if a number such as 575 was played,
there were only two other permutations (557 and 755), so
the bet on the box required only two units. Boxing a number like 555 makes no sense, so there you have it. A numbers runner picked the receipts up each morning and the
numbers for our outlet were thereby recorded.

Every afternoon around 5 P.M. I would call a newsroom
in central Erie and simply say, "What was it?" The number
would be recited, the line disconnected, and I would write
the number on a small slate board near the phone. When
our ladies called I was asked this same question. This was a
lot easier than repairing truck tires.

In his book *Scarne's New Complete Guide to Gambling*, John
Scarne describes the Numbers Racket and on pages 201–2
mentions the notion of a "cut number."[1] This is a number
that presumably gets heavy play since it is considered a lucky
number by many players (711 might be an example). As a
result the Numbers operator either paid this number at
smaller (cut) odds than other numbers or refused to accept
wagers on it at all. Though cut numbers did not occur in my
venue, I don't doubt that this happened in some. Scarne also
mentions that payoffs were typically 500 to 1 (meaning 499
to 1), though in my outlet the payoff was always 599 to 1.

The Numbers Racket no longer exists because many of the
state lotteries now have wagers that are either identical or
very similar to those offered by the mob. Ironically, the payoffs
on these state games are not as good as some of the payoffs

that were offered by the mob. On the other hand, the profits from state numbers games now go for education and other worthwhile state expenditures rather than into the pockets of hoodlums. In addition, as I'll describe in the next section, state lotteries today have the capability of linking games among several states, thereby creating games with huge payoffs. Not only would the mob be uncomfortable banking such games, but the publicity surrounding these games would also be a feature that would not sit well with gangsters.

Periodically, the morality of operating state lotteries is discussed by politicians, educators, and especially those who work in the field of addiction and compulsive behavior. They have some valid points. It is disturbing to see television and billboard promotions used by state government to entice people to spend money on games that, as I will show in chapter 3, are very poor bets. We will discuss this further in chapter 5 but for now, suffice it to say, if you oppose the state lottery, don't play it. If you do play it, then play it responsibly. If you buy a ticket then know that you aren't getting a very attractive wager. Nevertheless, if you can afford the loss, then at least you have a day or so to dream about what you'll do with all of that money if you win the big one; your own version of California Dreamin'.

The State Lottery Explosion

We have already discussed the birth of the New Hampshire State Lottery. Rather than failing as some had predicted, this lottery eventually flourished and soon other states created their own lotteries. It is interesting to observe the timeline vis-à-vis the geographic location of the states as their lotteries came into being. Here is a list of the current state lotteries operating in the United States and the year in which they were sanctioned. The list is in chronological order rather than alphabetical:

1964	New Hampshire	1988	District of Columbia
1967	New York		Florida
1970	New Jersey		Kansas
1972	Connecticut		Minnesota
	Michigan		Rhode Island
	Pennsylvania		West Virginia
1974	Maine	1989	Idaho
	Massachusetts		Indiana
	Ohio		Kentucky
1976	Delaware		South Dakota
1977	Vermont	1991	Louisiana
1981	Arizona		Virginia
1982	Washington	1992	Georgia
1983	Colorado		Texas
1984	Missouri	1995	New Mexico
1985	California	1996	Nebraska
	Iowa	1997	Maryland
1986	Illinois	2001	South Carolina
	Montana	2002	Tennessee
1987	Oregon		
	Wisconsin		

Clearly, the lottery phenomenon started in the Northeast and spread, though not uniformly, from adjoining state to adjoining state and eventually included the upper Midwest and the central Atlantic states. The birth in the Southwest started in Arizona then spread to Colorado and California and later to Texas and New Mexico. The northwest expansion started in Washington and then spread to Iowa, Oregon, Montana, Idaho, and Nebraska. The southeast consisted of Florida, Georgia, and eventually South Carolina; absent were Mississippi and Alabama, though Louisiana had returned to its lottery roots the year before Georgia joined. The states in the center of the country got it from all sides. The expansion was not completely uniform, but the above timeline does show the Primm Valley phenomenon at work. For a neat map of current lottery states go to the Minnesota lottery Web site *www.lottery.state.mn.us/overview/gambmap.gif.*

It is interesting to note the states that do not, as of writing, have lotteries:

Alaska	North Carolina
Alabama	North Dakota
Arkansas	Oklahoma
Hawaii	Utah
Mississippi	Wyoming
Nevada	

One quick way to make a book obsolete is to make predictions that later turn out to be wrong. Using the same good judgment that I did when I wrote numbers in that gas station back in Erie, I'll make some predictions anyway. I would have picked North Dakota as a state that would create a state lottery but in 1986 they voted against creating their own system, the first post–New Hampshire state to do so. This decision has stood for some 16 years, so I have placed them in the "no lottery" group. Although some states, such as Connecticut and California, have both casinos and lotteries, when the casinos are there first as in Nevada, the lotteries lose out. I therefore also placed Mississippi and Nevada in the "no lottery" group.*

Utah will remain without a state lottery because of the heavy Mormon influence in the state. Alaskans are content with their negative taxes due to oil, so I don't see a big push for a state lottery there. Hawaii, although it derives some revenues from agriculture and the military, produces most of its revenue from short-term tourism and I don't see tourists buying Hawaiian lottery tickets, especially for games that require cumulative jackpots. This leaves Alabama, Arkansas, North Carolina, Oklahoma, and Wyoming as states that I see as eventually adopting a state lottery. Of course some of these, like North Dakota, may surprise me.

A discussion of the evolution of state lotteries would be incomplete without mentioning the creation of the Multistate Lottery Corporation and its subsequent game, Powerball. Powerball has had a profound impact on the structure of state lottery games. Here's the story.

In September of 1987, five of the less populated states— Iowa, Kansas, Oregon, Rhode Island, and West Virginia— and the District of Columbia banded together to form the Multistate Lottery Corporation (MUSL). Shortly thereafter Missouri also joined the corporation. The purpose of the

* However, see the discussion of the Nevada Numbers game on page 89.

MUSL was to create bigger jackpots by building a larger player base. The seeds of this idea were probably planted by the creation of the Tri State Lottery in 1985 by the states of Maine, New Hampshire, and Vermont. The first game offered by MUSL, Lotto America, started operating during February of 1988. In Lotto America, players picked seven numbers from 40 and tried to match the lottery's seven picks. In the first six months of operation the game had sales of approximately $32 million, peanuts in lottery terms, and profits from this were split among the members of MUSL.

Approximately one year after Lotto America was launched, the game was changed to a pick-6-from-54 game with two plays for one dollar. This meant that the jackpot was harder to hit (1 chance in 25,827,165 per game) than the maiden version (1 chance in 18,643,560), but it also meant larger jackpots. This new version was somewhat successful, and by 1991 MUSL was enjoying annual sales in excess of four hundred million dollars. Part of this success, however, was simply due to the fact that MUSL membership had grown with the addition of Delaware, Idaho, Indiana, Kentucky, Maine, Minnesota, Montana, South Dakota, and Wisconsin. So, although revenues were up, MUSL members faced the same problems they had earlier: too much overhead for the revenue.

Noting that players seemed to want large jackpots with low stakes, MUSL ended the Lotto America game with a final draw on April 18, 1992, and immediately replaced it with a new game called Powerball. In Powerball, players picked five numbers, called white balls, from the numbers 1 to 45 and then picked an additional number, the red Powerball, from the same numbers 1 through 45. This meant, as we'll see in the next chapter, that the player's chances of picking a winning jackpot ticket (all five numbers plus the Powerball) were 1 in 54,979,155. Sales and revenues started well, but by 1997 there were again problems, in part because, by this time, several other states had joined MUSL. Although Maine had withdrawn (along with Georgia who had joined in 1995), Arizona, Connecticut, Louisiana, Nebraska, New Hampshire, and New Mexico were now on board. Something had to be done.

In November of 1997, Powerball was changed to a format in which the five white balls were picked from 49 numbers and the Powerball was picked from 42. This seems like a slight change but, as one can determine using calculations explained in the next chapter, it lowers the chances of getting the jackpot to 1 in 80,089,128. This revised system produced two jackpots of over one hundred million dollars during the first two months of operation, and annual sales jumped over the one-billion-dollar mark and have stayed there ever since. By July 29, 1996, the Powerball jackpot was over $295 million, the largest Powerball jackpot to date, and was won by a group that refers to itself as "the Lucky 13". You'll see why when I tell their story in chapter 4.

On October 9, 2002, one month after I thought I had finished writing this book, MUSL changed the white ball pool from 49 to 53, thereby lowering the chances of winning the Powerball jackpot to 1 in 120,526,770. Hopefully, by the time you read this the game will still have that format. At the present time there are 23 members in the MUSL corporation.

The Games

The previous section shows that 38 states, plus the District of Columbia, have lotteries. Each lottery has its own set of games with different names, different odds, and different payoffs. In an attempt to create order out of all of this information, I have classified the games into 15 general categories by way of their structure. The payoffs are not included in this categorization. You can find this information for a specific game by referring to the state lottery Web site; the URL for each is given in the appendix.

There were only four games that did not fit into my classifications. The first was a horseracing-type game in California called Daily Derby, the second a sports betting game in Oregon called Sports Action, the third a game in Wisconsin called City Picks, and the last a game in Indiana called Max Five. Information on Daily Derby can be found at *www.calottery.com/games/dailyderby/dailyderby.asp,* and information about Sports Action, a game only playable during football season, can be viewed at *www.oregonlottery.org/sports.* Because it was difficult to obtain technical information about California Derby and Sports Action I did not analyze either of them. Max Five, a Hoosier game that debuted on January 23, 2002, was short-lived and ended on January 12, 2003, so there was no point in analyzing that game either. I do analyze City Picks; from the point of view of mathematical analysis, it is one of the most interesting games I encountered.

Here are the categories of games, and their descriptions:

PICK FIVE + PICK ONE   This is a Powerball-type game in which the player picks five out of a group of numbers, plus one number (sometimes called a *power ball*) out of a separate group. The jackpot is won when all six numbers match the draw by the lottery. Other payoffs are based on combinations of the five and the one.

PICK FIVE ROLL DOWN   Here the player picks five numbers out of a group of numbers. The jackpot is won if the player matches all five picks with the lottery's picks; otherwise the jackpot is distributed among the lesser winning combinations (it is thus "rolled down").

PICK FOUR + PICK ONE   This is the same format as the Pick Five + Pick One except that it is somewhat easier to win.

PICK SIX + LB   Here the player picks six numbers from a group of numbers. When the lottery picks its six winning numbers it also picks a seventh number called a bonus number ("LB" stands for "lottery bonus") from the remaining group. The jackpot is won if the player's six numbers match the lottery's six numbers. If the player has five numbers plus the LB number the player wins second prize. Third prize is five of six and so on. In games like Mass Millions, LB only comes into play in determining the second prize, nothing else; in others it plays a role in the smaller prizes (for instance, Tri State Megabucks).

PICK SIX   This is just what you would think. The player and lottery each pick six numbers from the same group. Prizes depend upon how many of the lottery's numbers the player picked, usually at least three for a prize.

PICK SEVEN   Same as Pick Six except seven numbers are involved.

PICK FIVE   Same as Pick Six except only five numbers are involved.

PICK FIVE + LB   Same as Pick Six + LB but player only picks five.

PICK FOUR—TWO BY TWO   Player picks two numbers out of a group of red numbers, and then two more numbers out of a complete group of the same numbers, this time white. The lottery does the same. Payouts are based on matching four, three, two, or one numbers of any color with the lottery's numbers.

PICK FOUR DIGITS   Player picks four digits such as 2345. Lottery also picks four digits. For the biggest prize, the player must match the order of the four digits with the order of the lottery's pick. Depending on the venue, there are several other bets that a player can make, many of them depending upon boxing the number as I explained previously while discussing the Numbers Racket.

PICK THREE DIGITS   This is structured exactly like the Numbers Racket, except that the player can also play the front or back pair. For instance, if the number is 123, then the front-pair bet wins if the winning number is of the form 12x and the back pair bet wins if it is of the form x23.

DIGITS AND LETTERS   This latest group of new games was initiated by the states of Georgia and Michigan. The player picks four digits and two letters of the alphabet in a set order such as A1234B (Georgia) or AB1234 (Michigan). Player gets six such combinations from the lottery's computer and must match one of them with the lottery's draw, in exact order, to win.

GROUPS OF FOUR There are just a few of these games around—for instance, Oregon Win for Life, Louisiana Cash Quest, Washington Lucky for Life, and New Jersey Lotzee. The player either self-picks, or allows the lottery's computer to pick, four numbers from a complete set of numbers. The lottery computer then picks several more sets of four from the same set of numbers. These sets are arranged into groups with the player's choice of four being the only set in group 1, the rest being in groups 2, 3, and sometimes 4, the number of groups and the number of sets in each group depending upon the game in question. The lottery then picks four numbers from the original, full set of numbers, and prizes are awarded depending upon how many of these the player has and what group they are in. I'll explain this in more detail later.

KENO Keno, as I mentioned earlier, dates back to the Han Dynasty in China around 200 B.C. The game originally used as many as 120 Chinese characters, and is commonly believed to have been imported into the United States by the Chinese immigrants who helped construct railroads in the old West. Though it was illegal, it was enthusiastically played by these immigrants and became known as the Chinese Lottery. Sometime near the end of the 19th century the numbers 1 to 80 replaced the Chinese characters. When gambling was legalized in Nevada in 1931, lotteries were not covered by the legislation; it was at this point that the name "Chinese Lottery" was changed to "Horse Race Keno" and the game became legal. When the government passed a law taxing off-track betting, Nevada simply changed the name to Keno.

Keno was not part of state lotteries as they originated. In 1988, New York was the first state to introduce Keno as a state lottery game; and other states soon followed suit. The change probably required some additional state legislation, because Keno tickets were sold in saloons and restaurants rather than by lottery outlets.

In the game of Keno, the player can pick several numbers from the numbers 1 through 80 and mark them on a card. The lottery then picks 20 of the 80 numbers and prizes are awarded depending upon how many numbers the player picked and how many of these match the lottery's 20 picks.

SCRATCHERS These are scratch tickets and every lottery offers a variation of them. A general description is impossible since there are so many versions, and their payoff structure is not public knowledge. Nevertheless, I will give an

> example below of a typical
> Scratcher game that I myself
> played, and for which I did man-
> age to get the payoff structure.

This would be the logical place to list a description of which states offer which games, and what the games are called state by state. As page after page of this would be as interesting as a mashed potato sandwich, I am going to put that information in the appendix and you can refer to it, or not, as you see fit. Nevertheless, I should at least like to give some concrete examples of the above games, so you can see exactly how they work. I will also use these examples to show you how to compute the relevant statistics for each type of lottery game. Some of the games described below are multistate games, and a listing of all multistate games can be found on *www.lotteryamerica.com*. Although I'll refer back to these examples when I do lottery computations, you may want to give these a cursory reading on your first pass. Of course, I can't blame you for wanting to get on to all of the exciting mathematics in the next chapter.

Here are the examples:

> POWERBALL   This Pick Five + Pick One–format
> game is played in 21 states and
> D.C. The cost per play is one dol-
> lar. The player picks five white
> balls from the numbers 1 to 53,
> and one red Powerball from the

numbers 1 to 42. On the day of the draw the lottery randomly picks five white ball numbers from 1 to 53 and a Powerball number from 1 to 42. The payoff to the player is as follows:

5 white + PB	Jackpot
5 white	$100,000
4 white + PB	$5,000
4 white	$100
3 white + PB	$100
3 white	$7
2 white + PB	$7
1 white + PB	$4
PB only	$3

There is another option for the player. For an additional one dollar, the player can choose the Powerball Extra option. This involves the Powerball lottery randomly choosing a number 2 through 5, called a "multiplier." If the player has chosen the Powerball Extra option and wins a prize other than the jackpot, the prize is multiplied by the multiplier to determine the player's payoff.

If a player wins the jackpot it is either paid off in a 29-year annuity or in a lump-sum payment which is approximately half of the jackpot amount.

There is also a related *Powerball Instant Millionaire* show, but it is actually part of a scratch ticket game so I'll not pursue it here.

Another multistate Pick Five + Pick One game is Mega Millions, formerly known as the Big Game. It was changed by raising the pool of five numbers from 50 to 52 and the Pick One pool from 36 to 52. New pay tables can be found by referring to the Web site, *www.megamillions.com*.

SHOW ME FIVE PAYDOWN Until recently the principal game of this type was an MUSL game played in 10 states called Rolldown. The last Rolldown drawing was on April 6, 2002—while I was writing this section. The game was replaced by a Powerball-type game called Hot Lotto. There are still Rolldown-type games around—for instance, the Show Me Five Paydown from the state of Missouri, which is a Pick Five

Rolldown game. The cost to play is one dollar and the player chooses five numbers from 1 to 44. The lottery also draws five numbers from 1 to 44, some of which the player must match in order to win. If there is no jackpot winner the lower prizes are increased. Here is the pay table:

		No Jackpot
5 matches	$50,000	N/A
4 matches	$250	$750
3 matches	$10	$25
2 matches	Free play	$2

TRI STATE CASH LOTTO The Tri State Cash Lotto operated by Vermont, Maine, and New Hampshire is a Pick Four + Pick One type game. For one dollar the player picks four numbers from 1 to 33 plus a single, "Wild" number from 1 to 33. The Tri State Lottery does the same and the payoffs are as follows:

4 matches + Wild	$200,000
4 matches only	$2,000
3 matches + Wild	$200
3 matches only	$50
2 Matches + Wild	$20

2 matches only	$1
Wild	$2

In case there are more than three jackpot winners, they split $600,000 evenly.

TRI STATE MEGABUCKS The Tri State Megabucks, again played in Maine, New Hampshire, and Vermont, is a game of the Pick Six + LB type. For one dollar the player picks six numbers from 1 to 42. The Tri State Lottery randomly picks six in the same fashion and then picks an extra (Bonus) ball from the remaining 36. Here is the pay table:

6 matches	Jackpot
5 matches + Bonus	$10,000
5 matches	$1,000
4 matches + Bonus	$50
4 matches	$40
3 matches + Bonus	$5
2 matches + Bonus	$2
3 matches	$1

LOTTO SOUTH This is a Pick Six–type game that is played in Georgia, Kentucky, and Virginia. The player picks six numbers from 1 to 49; the Tri State Lottery does the same. The pay table is somewhat cryptic in that the winners below the jackpot are not fixed amounts but are advertised as *average* payouts. Here they are:

Match 6	Jackpot
Match 5	$1000 average
Match 4	$75 average
Match 3	$5 average

MARYLAND CASH IN HAND   This is a Pick Seven game. The player picks seven numbers from the group of numbers 1 to 31, and the lottery does the same. Drawings are held six days a week. Here is the payoff table:

Match 7	$500,000
Match 6	$1,000
Match 5	$40
Match 4	$4
Match 3	Free play

MASS CASH   This is a Pick Five game offered by Massachusetts. The player picks five numbers from 1 to 35 and the Massachusetts State Lottery does the same. Here is the pay table:

Match 5	$100,000
Match 4	$250
Match 3	$10

MASS MILLIONS   This is another Massachusetts game, this time of the type Pick Six + LB. The player picks six numbers from the numbers 1 to 49. The Massachusetts State Lottery does the same except that after they have chosen their six numbers they randomly pick one of the remaining 43 numbers to be a Bonus number. Here is the pay table:

Match 6	Jackpot
Match 5 + Bonus	$50,000
Match 5	$3,000
Match 4	$100
Match 3	Free bet

RHODE ISLAND   This is a Pick Five + LB–type
WILD MONEY   game. The player picks five numbers from the numbers 1 to 35. Every Tuesday, Thursday, and Saturday the Rhode Island Lottery

picks five numbers from 1 to 35 plus a bonus (Extra) ball from the remaining 30 numbers. There is a minimum $20,000 jackpot, and the pay table is as follows:

Match 5	Jackpot
Match 4 + Extra	$15,000
Match 4	$200
Match 3 + Extra	$50
Match 3	$5
Match 2 + Extra	$5

NEBRASKA TWO BY TWO This MUSL game is actually played in several states. The player picks two "red" numbers from 1 to 26, and two "white" numbers from 1 to 26, for a total of four numbers. The lottery does the same. The payoff table is as follows:

Match 4	$20,000
Match 3	$100
Match 2	$3
Match 1	Free play

Note that colors don't matter in the payoff structure. Drawings are Monday, Wednesday, and Saturday.

TRI STATE PICK FOUR   This is a Pick Four Digits game as played in New Hampshire, Maine, and Vermont. It is played daily. Some states have variations on the wagers stated here, but the New Hampshire straight and box bets are typical of all states. The player picks four digits, each from 0 to 9, in order. For example, 0753 could be a choice. The cost is 50¢. Box bets are the same as those described earlier when the Numbers Racket was discussed, namely, any permutation of the number wins. In case some numbers are repeated, these box bets have a higher payoff because fewer permutations are possible. For example, a number such as 1222 has only four distinct permutations and thus a box around such a number is called a *four-way box*. Here is the pay table:

Straight	$2500
4-way box	$625 (Ex. 1222)
6-way box	$417 (Ex. 1212)

12-way box $208 (Ex. 1223)

24-way box $104 (Ex. 1234)

Front pair $50 (Ex. 12xx)

Back pair $50 (Ex. xx12)

TRI STATE PICK THREE   This is the type of game that put the Numbers Racket out of business. This game, played in New Hampshire, Maine, and Vermont is almost identical to Pick Three–type games in other states. The player picks three digits, such as 456; the cost to play is 50¢. Here is the pay table:

Straight	$250
3-way box	$83 (Ex. 122)
6-way box	$42 (Ex. 123)
Front pair	$25 (Ex. 12x)
Back pair	$25 (Ex. x23)

You can also play the same number straight and boxed, but this is really just two separate bets.

LOUISIANA CASH QUEST   This is an example of what I called a Groups of Four game. It costs one dollar for each game. The player selects four numbers from the numbers 1 to 50 (or they can be chosen by a "quick pick" from the lottery computer). These four numbers are placed in a group called group 1. The lottery then picks six other sets of four numbers, each set of four is randomly chosen from the numbers 1 to 50. These six sets of numbers are then subdivided into two groups. Group 2 contains two of the sets of four and group 3 contains four of the sets of four. The result is a player ticket with three groups of four number sets, one set in group 1, two in group 2, and four in group 3. The lottery then randomly chooses four numbers from the numbers 1 to 50 (every Wednesday and Saturday) and the winners are paid by matching numbers according to the following pay table:

4 numbers from group 1	$50,000
One 4-number set from group 2	$3,000
One 4-number set from group 3	$500

Match 3 from any 1 set in any group	$10
Match 2 from any 1 set in any group	$1

If there are more than five winners in group 1 who match all four numbers, then they share $250,000 on a pari-mutuel basis.

N.Y. QUICK DRAW   This is a Keno game. Many states (such as Massachusetts) simply call their Keno game Keno. New York, however, calls its Keno game Quick Draw; California calls it Hot Spot. It's still Keno.[*]

The differences from state to state involve the pay tables and how many numbers the players are allowed to select. In New York, players can choose from one to 10 numbers from the a set of 1 through 80, in Massachusetts players can select up to 12 of these

---

[*] The California game has an added feature wherein the player, for an additional charge, picks an additional number called "Bulls Eye" from the 80 numbers. This number acts in the same fashion as a powerball, and the game can be so analyzed. The wager is only available on two-, three-, four-, and five-spot tickets.

numbers, and in California players can select two, three, four, five, or eight numbers. For clarity, let's suppose that the player chooses four numbers; this is called a four-spot game. The lottery then randomly chooses 20 of the numbers 1 to 80. The player is then paid according to how many of the player's four numbers match those of the lottery's 20. Here is the Quick Draw pay table for a one-dollar four-spot ticket:

Match 4	$55
Match 3	$5
Match 2	$1
Match 0 or 1	$0

Keno can generally be played in bars and restaurants and the game is repeated every four or five minutes depending upon the state (i.e., Georgia offers the game every four minutes and California every five). There are so many different pay tables from state to state that I am not going to attempt to list all of the games that are available. However, I will list Web sites in the appendix where you can find full details if you wish, and I will also give the house edge for four- and five-spot tickets. The reason I picked the Quick Draw four-spot game as an example will become apparent in the last chapter.

WINNER WONDERLAND: This Massachusetts scratch ticket was offered during the Christmas season of 2001, and is typical of the hundreds of scratch games available across the country, so I'll use it as the example of a scratch game.

The ticket costs five dollars. (Prices vary; a cheaper Massachusetts ticket was the two-dollar Holiday Cash ticket.) The player scratches an area of the ticket called "Winning Numbers" to reveal three numbers from among the numbers 1 through 20. There are then 10 places to scratch in an area called "Your Numbers." Again, each of these reveals a number from 1 to 20, a $$ symbol, or a picture of a snowflake, each with a prize amount. If the number you scratch matches one of the winning numbers, or is the $$ symbol, you win the prize specified, from $5 to $250,000. If you get a snowflake symbol on any one of your 10 numbers you win all 10 of the amounts specified under "Your Numbers." That's all there is to it. I'll have more to say about this game later.

POWERBALL
INSTANT MILLIONAIRE

MUSL offers one scratch game—Powerball Instant Millionaire. It is offered in some venues in which regular Powerball is available. Basically, players buy a Powerball Instant Millionaire scratch ticket and, as with all scratch tickets, can win money instantly. The big prize, however, is the entry symbol on the ticket that is sometimes found under the Bonus Ball. This entitles the ticket bearer to the following:

1. A trip for two to Las Vegas
2. Three free nights at the Venetian in Las Vegas
3. $750 in spending money

4. A chance to win $1,000 to $1,000,000 on the Instant Millionaire show at the Venetian

You can find more information about the game at *www.musl.com/pbim*.

You'll notice that in many of the above pay tables I listed the grand prize simply as "jackpot." This is because there is no fixed amount for these prizes. The amount depends upon a game's *handle*—the total amount wagered—and, in the case of progressive games, how many games have already been played with no big winner. We'll look at the details in the next chapter.

One final comment. You'll notice, as mentioned above, that while I was writing this book an MUSL game, Roll-down, was dropped and replaced with a game called Hot Lotto. Another interstate game, the Big Game, was dropped and replaced with a game called Mega Millions. I'll have more to say about these events in the last chapter.

3

Go Figure

Vig, Juice, Rake, Take or Hold—
It All Amounts to the Same Thing

In any gambling game that caters to the public, the game's operator, be it your neighborhood bookie or a large corporation such as a casino, racetrack, or state lottery, must take in more money than it pays out or the operation will soon go out of business. Although the five terms used in the title of this section have somewhat different technical meanings, they all refer to the portion of the money wagered that is kept by the game's operator and is not returned to the players. The most common way to express this idea is to speak of the *house edge*. The house edge is a theoretical percentage that attempts to predict the percentage of the total amount that is wagered on a given game that will be retained by the house (meaning the operator).

The actual percentage is, of course, easy to figure after the fact. Suppose that for some game with an obvious start and finish (these could simply be time limits for a continuously running game) there is a total of W dollars wagered. Of this, R dollars are retained by the house and P dollars are returned to the players as prizes. Obviously the fraction R/W expressed as a percentage is the actual percentage of the wagers retained by the house. It is clear that $W \geq R$ (the symbol $\geq$ is shorthand for the phrase "is greater than or equal to") since the house can't take more away from the players than the amount that the players wager. Ostensibly, P is the difference between these two, that is:

$$P = W - R \qquad (1)$$

is the amount of money not retained by the house; in other words it is the portion of W returned to the players. Rearranging (1) we have:

$$W = P + R \qquad (2)$$

Now there is no restriction that keeps the players from winning more than they wager, that is, we can have $P > W$. In fact, this is exactly the situation that all players hope for. Since, by (2), $R = W - P$, the condition $P > W$ means that the house has a negative retention. In other words the house has to cough up enough money to cover the player's winnings. A successful gambling operation is one in which this doesn't happen or at least doesn't happen very often. All of which brings us back to the house edge.

Let us suppose that we have a *Wheel of Fortune*–type game. That is, the player makes a $1 wager, spins the wheel, and is paid (or not) according to where the wheel stops. Assume that the wheel has 40 stops and each stop (by symmetry) is equally likely. Stop number 1 returns $8 to the player; stops 20 and 40 return $4 to the player; stops 5, 10, 15, 25, and 30 return $2 to the player; stops 2, 8, 14, 16, 21, 23, 27, 29, 31, 33, 36, and 38 each return $1 to the player; and the remaining stops return nothing. Suppose that we play this game 40 times and each of the 40 numbers comes up exactly once. It is unlikely that this would actually happen, of course, but if we did this experiment 4 billion times we would expect the ratio of each number occurring to the total number of plays would be close to $\frac{1}{40}$. In other words this is a theoretical experiment. It is what would happen if these equally likely stops did, in fact, occur equally. The belief here is that in a large number of trials the wheel would approximate such behavior.

FIGURE 1
Example Showing Expected Return to Player

OUTCOME	FREQUENCY	PAYOUT	PRODUCT
Return 8	1	8	8
Return 4	2	4	8
Return 2	5	2	10
Return 1	12	1	12
Return 0	20	0	0
Total	40	—	38

Very well, our theoretical wager W is $40. The return to the player can be calculated by taking the number of stops for a given payout and multiplying it by that payout amount.

The total of these numbers will be the theoretical return to the player P. This calculation can be carried out systematically by using a table such as in figure 1. According to this table the theoretical return to the player P is \$38. Thus, applying relation (2), the retention by the house is \$40 − \$38 or \$2. The house edge is, therefore, $\frac{2}{40}$—or, expressed as a percentage, 5 percent. In other words, in the long run we would expect that the house would keep approximately five percent of all money wagered on this game. It should be noted that the number $\frac{38}{40}$ expressed as a percentage (95 percent) represents the theoretical return to the player and that $5\% + 95\% = 100\%$. This is no coincidence. Dividing both sides of (2) by W and multiplying by 100 it is easy see that

$$\textit{Percent return to player} + \textit{House edge} = 100 \qquad (3)$$

It is customary for casinos and lotteries to speak of the return to the player rather than the house edge, since in their collective mind it seems to put things in a more positive perspective. Obviously, by (3), either statistic determines the other. Whenever the theoretical percentage return to the player is larger than 100 percent this is called a *positive game* (for the player). Whenever the return to the player is less than 100 percent the game is called a *negative game;* when the return is exactly 100 percent the game is called a *fair game.*

I should note that, rather than carrying out the calculation in figure 1 we could have divided each of the entries in the frequency column by 40, multiplied each of these by the corresponding payout, and added the results. The answer would be exactly what we calculated from figure 1, namely, $\frac{38}{40}$. The numbers resulting from dividing the frequencies by the total number of stops are called *probabilities*. Thus, in the row corresponding to "Return 2" the number $\frac{5}{40}$, or what is the same, $\frac{1}{8}$, would be interpreted as saying that we would expect, on average, that a return of two would occur one-eighth of the time.

Although this is conceptually nice, it turns out that the probabilities involved in lottery calculations are so tiny that round-off errors can degrade calculations. Lotteries themselves recognize that probabilities are inconvenient and so they use the notion of chances. The above probability would be described by a lottery as 1 chance in 8 and written as 1:8.[*] This is acceptable unless the probability does not reduce to the form $\frac{1}{n}$. For example, the fraction $\frac{12}{40}$ corresponding to the "Return 1" event reduces to $\frac{1}{3.3333}$ . . . , which some lotteries would simply round to 1:3; it is not really correct. The point here is that most of my calculations will be of the form in figure 1. That is to say, I will usually find the total number of possible outcomes (the 40 in our example) and then find the number of these that correspond to each of the winning, or losing, events (the frequencies). Once this is accomplished the return to the player will be calculated just as was done in figure 1. In a couple of instances I will opt for probabilities instead. All of this is a bit harder than it sounds because, as we will see, the numbers involved in lottery games are very,

[*] Many lotteries refer to this as "odds," which is not really correct. One chance in eight is really one-to-seven odds in favor or seven-to-one odds against. Even this can be misleading, since "odds" really refers to payoffs rather than chances, and a conversion from probability to odds or vice versa assumes a fair game. The concept of odds is best left for discussion another day; I'll stick with chances.

very large; one runs out of fingers and toes in a hurry. The next section addresses this issue.

One Fish, Two Fish, Red Fish, Blue Fish

Anyone with young children will recognize the title of this section; you may well have the whole book committed to memory. Counting is one of the first skills we acquire after learning to say "Mama" and "Papa" and a few other words that strike our early fancy. It is an intrinsically human ability and activity, part of our everyday lives. Yet, I don't think there is a mathematician in the world who would take issue with the assertion that the counting of finite sets (sets with a finite number of elements) is a tricky and often difficult task. It is easy to be blindsided by this because the question posed in addressing most counting problems can usually be stated and understood by anyone, mathematician or not. Fortunately for us, the counting problems involved in studying lotteries are well known and easily understood. Nevertheless, even in this rather benign counting atmosphere we must use care because it is still easy to make a mistake.

Let me illustrate this with an example. The Multistate Lottery Corporation states (correctly) that in its Powerball game the chances of getting *only* a Powerball are 1:70.39. Yet, according to Bret Toyne, Assistant Executive Director/CFO of MUSL, each year approximately a dozen people write or call MUSL and assert that the figure is wrong. They argue that since there are 42 powerballs the correct figure should be 1:42. Their glib appraisal of the problem does not take into account that this equation requires not only that the correct Powerball be chosen, *but also* that none of the winning white balls be chosen. We'll look at the correct analysis below.

In order to do our counting properly we are going to need four counting principles, which I will simply label I through IV. In all candor, principles I and III will simply be used to obtain number IV but, hey, that's the way mathematics works; we try to break problems down into bites that we can chew. I've often told students of mine that the reason mathematics exists is that we humans are not all that bright, and we need mental tools to help us get to the truth. Here is number I:

Counting Principle I

If you count the number of elements in a finite set in two different ways then *you damn well better get the same answer in both instances.*

The idea here is that if you calculate the number of cows in a pen by counting their heads, and then later count their legs and divide by four, you had better end up with the same number in both cases. Though my example may sound silly it should also make sense to you.

In order to state the second of our counting principles in a concise fashion I'll need a bit of notation. If A and B are finite sets, then the set of all ordered pairs consisting of an element of A paired with an element of B, in that order, is denoted as $A \times B$. A simple example will help with this. Suppose that $A = \{a, b, c, d\}$ so that A consists of four elements. Further suppose that $B = \{1, 2\}$ so that B consists of two elements. An ordered pair consisting of an element x in A and an element y in B will be denoted simply as (x, y). Thus we have

$$A \times B = \{(a, 1), (b,1), (c, 1), (d, 1), (a, 2), (b, 2),$$
$$(c, 2)\ (d, 2)\} \tag{4}$$

One more piece of notation and we're all set. I'll denote the number of elements in a set S by the symbol $\#(S)$. In the above example $\#(A) = 4$ and $\#(B) = 2$.

Counting Principle II

If A and B are finite sets, then

$$\#(A \times B) = \#(A)\#(B) \tag{5}$$

In the example above we would have

$$\#(A \times B) = \#(A)\#(B) = 4 \cdot 2 = 8 \tag{6}$$

Notice that in (4) there are indeed eight elements in the set $A \times B$.

The second counting principle should seem natural to you. If there are m ways to choose an element in set A and n ways to choose an element in B, then *for each choice* in A there are n choices in B. Adding up all of these we get n added up m times which is just $m \cdot n$.

The second counting principle easily generalizes. If we have three finite sets A, B, and C then $A \times B \times C$ would represent the set of all ordered triples consisting of an element of A followed by an element of B and that followed by an element of C. This understood, (5) generalizes to

$$\#(A \times B \times C) = \#(A) \cdot \#(B) \cdot \#(C) \qquad (7)$$

In using (5) and (7) we will often use variations of the words "choice" and "choose" along with the notion of an "outcome," the outcome being an outcome in a lottery game. For example, if there are m ways of choosing three winning balls in a five-ball lottery game and there are n ways of choosing two losing balls in the game, then according to (5) there are $m \cdot n$ ways of choosing exactly three winning balls and two losing balls. Finding the m and n is another matter and that is where the next two counting principles come into play.

For the third counting principle we will need the notion of a *permutation*. A permutation is simply an ordering of several objects. A running example will be helpful here. Suppose that you are an art curator in a museum, and on a particular wall you have room for four paintings. If you have four paintings available to hang, then a particular choice of hanging them from left to right would comprise a permutation of the paintings. Now the first question is, how many permutations of these four paintings are there? The answer can be determined quite easily as follows. Think of the spots on which you can hang the paintings as being represented by four boxes from left to right:

Box 1	Box 2	Box 3	Box 4

Now how many ways can you fill in Box 1? Obviously there are four choices. Once such a choice has been made, you need to determine how many ways Box 2 can be filled. Since one of the paintings is already hung, there are three paintings left so there are clearly three choices for Box 2. Now for *each* of the four choices you make in Box 1 you can make three choices for Box 2, so altogether there are 4 · 3 or 12 ways that Box 1 and Box 2 can be filled in. This argument looks similar to that in counting principle II, and it is similar, but it is not exactly the same situation. In counting principle II the two (or more) sets were fixed. Here the second set (three paintings) depends upon which painting was selected from the original set of four paintings. Nevertheless, I think you can see that the product 4 · 3 is the correct calculation for the number of ways to fill in boxes 1 and 2. This done, for each of the 12 ways to fill in boxes 1 and 2 there are two ways left to fill in Box 3, so altogether there are 12 · 2 or 24 ways to fill in boxes 1, 2, and 3. Notice that once the first three boxes are filled there is only one choice for the painting that goes into Box 4 so there are 24 · 1 or 24 ways to fill in all four boxes. Let me summarize. There are 4 · 3 · 2 · 1 or 24 permutations of four objects.

What if we had n paintings and n wall spaces? I think that it is easy to see that in this case the number of permutations would be the product $n \cdot (n - 1) \cdot (n - 2) \ldots 3 \cdot 2 \cdot 1$. We will denote this number by P_n^n. Mathematicians have a shorthand symbol for the above product; it is $n!$ and is read "n factorial." Let's make that official:

$$n! = n \cdot (n - 1) \cdot (n - 2) \ldots 3 \cdot 2 \cdot 1; n > 0 \qquad (8)$$

It follows, therefore, that using this notation we have

$$P_n^n = n! \qquad (9)$$

In our art museum example we showed that $P_4^4 = 4! = 24$.

The result that we are after, and that will call counting principle III, is a generalization of the result in (9). Here goes.

Let us now suppose that we have the same four spaces on the museum wall, but instead of just four paintings we have seven. How many different arrangements can we make? The analysis is just like that above. There are seven ways to fill in Box 1 and for each of these choices there are six ways to fill in Box 2. Altogether, then, there are $7 \cdot 6$ ways to fill in the first two boxes. This done, there are five ways to fill in Box 3 so altogether there are $7 \cdot 6 \cdot 5$ ways to fill in the first three boxes. Finally, there are four ways to fill in Box 4 so altogether there are $7 \cdot 6 \cdot 5 \cdot 4$ or 840 different ways to arrange the seven paintings in the four spots. We would call this the "number of permutations of seven objects taken four at a time." The symbol for this is P_4^7. As we see in (10), this number can be written using factorials:

$$P_4^7 = 7 \cdot 6 \cdot 5 \cdot 4 = \frac{7 \cdot 6 \cdot 5 \cdot 4 \cdot 3 \cdot 2 \cdot 1}{3 \cdot 2 \cdot 1} = \frac{7!}{3!} \qquad (10)$$

If we had five spaces available for the seven paintings the number of permutations would be P_5^7, which is $7 \cdot 6 \cdot 5 \cdot 4 \cdot 3$ or, using factorials, $\frac{7!}{2!}$ Noting that $3 = 7 - 4$ and $2 = 7 - 5$ we can write $P_4^7 = \frac{7!}{(7-4)!}$ and $P_5^7 = \frac{7!}{(7-5)!}$ so that the right hand side of the equality is expressed in terms of the numbers appearing on the left. Noting this, it is clear that we can generalize the above example to n objects permuted k at a time and this generalization is the third counting principle.

Counting Principle III

The number of permutations of n objects taken k at a time, written P_k^n where $k < n$, is given by the formula

$$P_k^n = \frac{n!}{(n-k)!} \qquad (11)$$

There is a technical problem here. If $k = n$ then the bottom of the fraction is 0!. We already know from (9) that the correct answer in this case is $n!$, so in order to make everything work out properly we extend the definition in (8) to 0 and *define* 0! = 1. This done, formula (11) holds for all k with $k \le n$.

Hang in there—we're just about done. Suppose now that we envision the following scenario. Our seven paintings are stored in a warehouse across town from the museum. In order to produce a particular permutation of four of these paintings on the museum wall we do the following. We first select four paintings and load them into a van. At this point the ordering doesn't matter as all we did was select four paintings. Now I don't know how many ways there are to do this so I will just introduce a symbol to represent the number. The standard symbol for this is $\binom{7}{4}$ and is called the number of *combinations* of seven objects taken four at a time. Once the four paintings are selected we drive them to the museum, unload them, and take them to be hung. Notice that now we have four objects that are to be hung in four spots, and we know from the above discussion on permutations that there are 4! ways to do this. So, there are $\binom{7}{4}$ ways to choose four paintings from seven, and *each time* this is done there are 4! ways to order them. In other words the number of permutations of seven things taken four at a time, is the number of ways to choose four paintings from seven times the number of ways to permute the four that were chosen. In symbols

$$P_4^7 = \binom{7}{4}4! \tag{12}$$

Now here is where we use counting principle I. We have counted P_4^7 in two different ways, one way represented by (11) and the other by (12). According to our first counting principle these must be equal, that is, we must have

$$\binom{7}{4}4! = \frac{7!}{(7-4)!} \tag{13}$$

Aha! We can solve equation (13) for $\binom{7}{4}$ and obtain

$$\binom{7}{4} = \frac{7!}{4!(7-4)!} \tag{14}$$

I think you can see that the above argument easily generalizes to n paintings and k choices. Which brings us to the fourth and last counting principle:

Counting Principle IV

The number of combinations of n things taken k at a time, written $\binom{n}{k}$, is given by the formula

$$\binom{n}{k} = \frac{n!}{k!(n-k)!} \tag{15}$$

Let's give it a try and see if it works. Suppose that set A consists of four elements:

$$A = \{a, b, c, d\} \tag{16}$$

The collection C of all two element sets we can form using the things in A is:

$$C = \{\{a, b\}, \{a, c\}, \{a, d\}, \{b, c\}, \{b, d\}, \{c, d\}\} \qquad (17)$$

which has six two-element sets. Checking our formula in this example we have:

$$\binom{4}{2} = \frac{4!}{2!(4-2)!} = \frac{4!}{2!\,2!} = \frac{4 \cdot 3}{2} = 6 \qquad (18)$$

and six is exactly right. Try five elements three at a time; you should get 10 three-element sets.

That's it! We have all the counting principles that we will need. In the next section you'll see how useful these counting principles are.

The Buck Stops Here, Well, Most of the Time

In this section I am going to use the principles that we just derived to look at some of the games mentioned in the previous chapter. I'll start with the easier games and work up to the harder ones. Once you understand the above principles, however, none of these games (except one) are really hard. Our goal here is to see just what the house edge is in some typical lottery games. Moreover, in games where there is a progressive jackpot we'll see just how big that jackpot needs to be to present the player with a positive game.

New York's Four-Spot Quick Draw

You will recall that, in a four-spot Keno game, the player picks four numbers out of the numbers 1 through 80. From our fourth counting principle there are $\binom{80}{4}$ ways to do this. Evaluating this expression we have:

$$\binom{80}{4} = \frac{80!}{4!(80-4)!} = \frac{80 \cdot 79 \cdot 78 \cdot 77 \cdot 76 \cdot 75 \ldots}{4 \cdot 3 \cdot 2 \cdot 1 \cdot 76 \cdot 75 \ldots} \quad (19)$$

which reduces to

$$\binom{80}{4} = \frac{80 \cdot 79 \cdot 78 \cdot 77}{4 \cdot 3 \cdot 2 \cdot 1} = 20 \cdot 79 \cdot 13 \cdot 77 = 1,581,580 \quad (20)$$

Altogether, then, there are 1,581,580 ways that one can select four numbers from an 80-number Keno ticket. Next, the New York Lottery selects 20 numbers from the 80 which divides the 80 numbers into two sets, a set of 20 "winners" and a set of 60 "losers." How many ways can a player select four winners and no losers? Easy, that number is just $\binom{20}{4}$, which is 4,845. How many ways can the player select exactly three winners and one loser? Well, there are $\binom{20}{3}$ ways to select three winners out of 20 and there are $\binom{60}{1}$ ways to select one loser out of 60. According to counting principle II the number of ways to select three winners *and* one loser is the product $\binom{20}{3}\binom{60}{1}$. This number is:

$$\binom{20}{3}\binom{60}{1} = \frac{20 \cdot 19 \cdot 18}{3 \cdot 2 \cdot 1} \cdot 60 = 68,400 \quad (21)$$

Similarly two winners and two losers is $\binom{20}{2}\binom{60}{2}$ or 336,300; one winner and three losers is $\binom{20}{1}\binom{60}{3}$ or 684,400; and four losers is $\binom{20}{0}\binom{60}{4}$ or 487,635.

With the above numbers in hand we can construct the following table, which is analogous to that in figure 1.

FIGURE 2
Player Return on Four-Spot Quick Draw

OUTCOME	FREQUENCY	PAYOUT	PRODUCT
4 Hits	4,845	55	266,475
3 Hits	68,400	5	342,000
2 Hits	336,300	1	336,300
1 Hit	684,400	0	0
0 Hits	487,635	0	0
Total	1,581,580	—	944,755

The fractional return to the player is $\frac{944,775}{1,581,580}$ or 0.5974. The percentage return to the player is, therefore, 59.74 percent, so the house edge is 40.26 percent. Notice that the frequencies we calculated add up correctly to the total number of ways to mark the four-spot ticket. This is always a good check on your calculations and is an example of counting principle I.

Before we leave this game note that if we add up the frequencies for two, three, and four hits the total is 409,545. If we divide this by 1,581,580 the result is 0.25895; this represents the probability of hitting *either* two, three, or four matches. The reciprocal of this number is approximately 3.86, which represents a 1 in 3.86 chance of getting these outcomes. The New York State Lottery advertises this as the chance of winning this bet (the Massachusetts State Lottery pulls the same stunt).

Wait a minute! I don't see any win when two matches occur; the one-dollar payout would be a *push*, since it cost one dollar to play. One in 3.86 is the chance of *not losing*; the chance of winning is 1 in 21.59. Many lotteries that have payouts equal to the price of the wager put such a payout in the "win" column and state the probability of winning accordingly. *Caveat gamblor!*

Tri State Pick Three

This game is so easily analyzed that you don't really need any counting principles. Since the payoffs listed on page 40 are for a 50¢ wager, they need to be doubled to put them on a per-dollar basis. There are one thousand choices of three ordered digits (000 to 999) and the payoff is 500 to 1. The return to the player is 50 percent, so the house edge is also 50 percent. For a six-way box the payoff is $84 for a one-dollar wager, so the return to the player is 6 · 84 or $504 for $1,000. The return to the player is thus 50.4 percent and the house edge is 49.6 percent. There are 10 ways to win a front-pair wager at $50 per one dollar wagered, so the return to the player is $500 per $1,000 wagered or a 50 percent return. All of the returns in this game are right around 50 percent.

Tri State Pick Four

As in the Tri State Pick Three above, all of these wagers hover right around the 50 percent return figure. I'll leave it to you to check this out.

Missouri's Show Me Five Paydown

Recall that in this game the player picks five numbers from 1 to 44 and the Missouri State Lottery does the same. There are two separate pay tables depending upon whether or not the $50,000 grand prize is won. Once the lottery chooses its five numbers the pool of 44 numbers is partitioned into a set of 5 winners and 39 losers. The frequencies are then easily obtained using our counting principles: $\binom{5}{5}\binom{39}{0}$ for five matches, $\binom{5}{4}\binom{39}{1}$ for four matches, $\binom{5}{3}\binom{39}{2}$ for three matches, $\binom{5}{2}\binom{39}{3}$ for two matches, $\binom{5}{1}\binom{39}{4}$ for one match, and $\binom{5}{0}\binom{39}{5}$ for no matches. These numbers are, respectively: 1; 195; 7,410; 91,390; 411,255; and 575,757. The number of ways to pick five numbers from 44 is $\binom{44}{5}$ and that number is 1,086,008. The only thing that makes the game a bit difficult is that the payoff for two matches is a free play. It would be wrong to count this as one dollar, because you don't have the option of cashing in the free play for that amount; you must take the play. The value of the free play is simply the fractional return of the game. This number can be easily computed using a bit of algebra. Just use x for the fractional return and enter this in the 2 Matches row under the Payout column in a table such as that in figure 3. The total payout for three, four, and five matches is 173,460 and the payout for two matches is $91,390x$. Completing the player return computation yields the equation

$$\frac{173,460 + 91,390 \cdot x}{1,086,008} = x \qquad (22)$$

The solution to (22) is $x = 0.174$. Here is the completed table:

FIGURE 3

Return on Missouri Show Me Five Paydown
with Grand Prize

OUTCOME	FREQUENCY	PAYOUT	PRODUCT
5 Matches	1	50,000.000	50,000
4 Matches	195	250.000	48,750
3 Matches	7,410	10.000	74,410
2 Matches	91,390	0.174	15,902
0 or 1 Matches	987,012	0.00	0
Total	1,086,008	—	189,062

Dividing 189,062 by 1,086,008 we obtain 0.17409, which is consistent with our 17.4 percent calculation. If there is no five-match winner the payout structure changes, as we see in the following table:

FIGURE 4

Return on Missouri Show Me Five Paydown
with no Grand Prize

OUTCOME	FREQUENCY	PAYOUT	PRODUCT
4 Matches	195	750.00	146,250
3 Matches	7,410	25.00	185,250
2 Matches	91,390	2.00	182,780
0 or 1 Matches	987,012	0.00	0
Total	1,086,007	—	514,280

Here if we divide 514,280 by 1,086,007 the result is 0.47355, so the return figure is approximately 47.4 percent. For those of you who are purists, the above frequencies divided by

1,086,007 represent conditional probabilities of each outcome given that no grand prize is awarded. In any case it should be clear to you that anyone playing this game is seriously hoping that there is no grand prize winner!

Mass Cash

Here the player picks five numbers from 1 to 35 and the lottery does the same. By now you should be able to calculate the frequencies. Just remember that, once the lottery picks its five numbers, the 35 original choices are partitioned into two sets, comprising 5 winners and 30 losers. If you do your calculations correctly you should obtain this table:

FIGURE 5
Mass Cash Return to Player

OUTCOME	FREQUENCY	PAYOUT	PRODUCT
5 Matches	1	100,000	100,000
4 Matches	150	250	30,000
3 Matches	4,350	10	43,500
0, 1, or 2 Matches	320,131	0	0
Total	324,632	—	173,500

Note that $\binom{35}{5}$ = 324,632, so our frequencies check. If we divide 173,500 by 324,632 the result is 0.534451, so the percentage payback on this game is approximately 53.45 percent. From other states I have investigated, I suspect that a portion of the 46.55 percent house edge is kept in a reserve fund, in case the number of payouts for a particular game is unusually large. However, I don't have specific details about this for Mass Cash.

Tri State Megabucks

In Tri State Megabucks, the jackpot is rolled if there is no winner. In some cases these games are difficult to analyze because it is unclear from looking at the growing jackpot just exactly how much of the handle is being applied to the jackpot. However, from looking at Web sites provided by the states offering this game, the payoff structure becomes quite clear.

Recall that this is a Pick Six + LB–type game. The player picks six numbers from 1 to 42. The lottery also picks six numbers from 1 to 42, and then picks an additional number, the Bonus number, from the remaining 36 numbers. (The pay table is given on page 35.) Notice that, once the lottery picks its numbers, the 42 numbers are partitioned into three classes, six of which are "winners," one of which is the Bonus number, and the remaining 35 being designated "losers". Here are the frequency computations:

6 winners -	$\binom{6}{6}\binom{1}{0}\binom{35}{0}$	=	1
5 winners + B -	$\binom{6}{5}\binom{1}{1}\binom{35}{0}$	=	6
5 winners -	$\binom{6}{5}\binom{1}{0}\binom{35}{1}$	=	210
4 winners + B -	$\binom{6}{4}\binom{1}{1}\binom{35}{1}$	=	525
4 winners -	$\binom{6}{4}\binom{1}{0}\binom{35}{2}$	=	8,925
3 winners + B -	$\binom{6}{3}\binom{1}{1}\binom{35}{2}$	=	11,900
3 winners -	$\binom{6}{3}\binom{1}{0}\binom{35}{3}$	=	130,900
2 winners + B -	$\binom{6}{2}\binom{1}{1}\binom{35}{3}$	=	98,175
2 winners -	$\binom{6}{2}\binom{1}{0}\binom{35}{4}$	=	785,400
1 winners + Anything	$\binom{6}{1}\binom{36}{5}$	=	2,261,952
no winners	$\binom{6}{0}\binom{36}{6}$	=	1,947,792
		Total =	5,245,786

You'll note that the total number of player choices is $\binom{42}{6}$, which is exactly 5,245,786; the frequencies look correct. Also note that the losers are the last three items listed above, so that the frequency of losers is the sum of the last three frequencies listed. That number is 4,995,144. With these numbers in hand we can construct the following table:

FIGURE 6
Tri State Megabucks Return to Player

OUTCOME	FREQUENCY	PAYOUT	PRODUCT
6 Matches	1	Jackpot	JP
5 Matches + B	6	10,000	60,000
5 Matches	210	1,000	210,000
4 Matches + B	525	50	25,250
4 Matches	8,925	40	357,000
3 Matches + B	11,900	5	59,500
2 Matches + B	98,175	2	196,350
3 Matches	130,900	1	130,900
Losers	4,995,144	0	0
Total	5,245,786	—	JP + 1,039,000

According to the New Hampshire Tri State Megabucks rules 4 and 5, the beginning jackpot prize is a minimum of $500,000 annualized in 25 payments. This means that the beginning jackpot prize pool requires $295,973 to fund this annuity (see my discussion of annuities later in this chapter). The prize pool is 50 percent of total sales, so in a theoretical game of 5,245,786 players the prize pool would be half of this, or $2,622,893. Of this $1,039,000 would go to pay off the non-jackpot winners (see figure 6), which leaves $1,583,893 for the jackpot. In terms of percentages, the jackpot is about 30.19 percent of total sales, so $980,368 in sales would have to occur before the minimum $500,000 prize could be covered (980,368 · 0.3019 = 295,973). Whether the jackpot stays constant until this number of sales is realized, or whether some other procedure is followed, is unclear to me, but I'm sure the procedure is either this or something similar.* I do know that there is a Tri State contingency fund to cover a situation wherein a jackpot occurs before sufficient funds have been collected to cover the jackpot. The above numbers are, of course, theoretical. The reality is that the lottery takes half of actual sales, subtracts the non-jackpot prizes, and puts the rest in the jackpot pool.

Notice that when the jackpot is rolled over several times, it gives the players an average return in excess of 100 percent as soon as it exceeds $4,206,786 as a lump sum payment. This is because $4,206,786 + $1,039,000 = $5,245,786, which is 100 percent of theoretical sales. The key word here is "average," and I'll have more to say about this in the last chapter.

Powerball

As pointed out in chapter 2, this MUSL game is of the type Pick Five + Pick One—not surprisingly, a Powerball-type game. The player picks five "white balls" from the numbers 1

---

* Also see the Nevada Numbers discussion on page 89 for a similar analysis.

to 53, and then picks a red "Powerball" number from the numbers 1 to 42. Altogether then, the player has $\binom{53}{5}\binom{42}{1}$ or 120,526,770 choices. The chance of winning the jackpot in this game is, therefore, 1 in 120,526,770, much smaller than the chances in the Megabucks game just described. To give you some idea just how large the number of choices is, if you traveled 120,526,770 miles in space you would have traveled a distance that is over 100 percent of the distance from the Earth to the sun!

The rules and payoffs for Powerball are given in chapter 2 on page 31. The calculations for the game are very similar to those we just did for the Tri State Megabucks. That is to say, here we have four sets of numbers: five winning white balls, 48 losing white balls, one winning red ball (the Powerball), and 41 losing red balls. Here are the calculations:

5 White + PB	$\binom{5}{5}\binom{48}{0}\binom{1}{1}\binom{41}{0}$	=	1
5 White	$\binom{5}{5}\binom{48}{0}\binom{1}{0}\binom{41}{1}$	=	41
4 White + PB	$\binom{5}{4}\binom{48}{1}\binom{1}{1}\binom{41}{0}$	=	240
4 White	$\binom{5}{4}\binom{48}{1}\binom{1}{0}\binom{41}{1}$	=	9,840
3 White + PB	$\binom{5}{3}\binom{48}{2}\binom{1}{1}\binom{41}{0}$	=	11,280
3 White	$\binom{5}{3}\binom{48}{2}\binom{1}{0}\binom{41}{1}$	=	462,480
2 White + PB	$\binom{5}{2}\binom{48}{3}\binom{1}{1}\binom{41}{0}$	=	172,960
2 White	$\binom{5}{2}\binom{48}{3}\binom{1}{0}\binom{41}{1}$	=	7,091,360
1 White + PB	$\binom{5}{1}\binom{48}{4}\binom{1}{1}\binom{41}{0}$	=	972,900
1 White	$\binom{5}{1}\binom{48}{4}\binom{1}{0}\binom{41}{1}$	=	39,888,900
0 White + PB	$\binom{5}{0}\binom{48}{5}\binom{1}{1}\binom{41}{0}$	=	1,712,304
0 White	$\binom{5}{0}\binom{48}{5}\binom{1}{0}\binom{41}{1}$	=	70,204,464
		Total =	120,526,770

Notice that the entry for 0 White + PB—namely, 1,712,304—divided by 120,526,770 is equal to approximately 70.38865 or about a 1:70.39 chance. This is the calculation that I alluded to on page 53. Here is the table showing the calculation of the player's average return in Powerball:

FIGURE 7

Average Player Return in Powerball

OUTCOME	FREQUENCY	PAYOUT	PRODUCT
5 White + PB	1	Jackpot	JP
5 White	41	100,000	4,100,000
4 White + PB	240	5,000	1,200,000
4 White	9,840	100	984,000
3 White + PB	11,280	100	1,128,000
3 White	462,480	7	3,237,360
2 White + PB	172,960	7	1,210,720
1 White + PB	972,900	4	3,891,600
PB Only	1,712,304	3	5,136,912
Losers	117,184,724	0	0
Total	120,526,770	—	JP + 20,888,592

The figure 20,888,592 divided by 120,526,770, and expressed as a percentage is approximately 17.33 percent, the average amount needed to pay off non-jackpot winners. According to its current Web site, MUSL actually budgets 21 percent of lottery receipts to pay off non-jackpot winners, a figure that I believe was determined when the white ball pool was 1 to 49. The jackpot in this game starts at $10,000,000 and increases a minimum of $2,000,000 for each succeeding draw. MUSL also retains an emergency fund that is collected by deducting a percentage of sales from the grand prize pool when certain circumstances arise. This fund is used to augment payoffs whenever there are an unusually large number of winners. In case the cash reserve fund is completely depleted, winners are paid off from 21 percent of the current wagers in a pari-mutuel fashion. According to MUSL this has never happened in the history of the game. MUSL administrative costs, which are less than 0.2 percent of Powerball sales, are billed to the participating states annually.

MUSL budgets 29 percent of receipts for the jackpot. This means that on average 50 percent (29% + 21%) of the wagers are returned to the players and 50 percent is retained by the states. Jackpots are rolled over and are increased using the 29 percent figure or $2,000,000, whichever is larger. Whenever the lump sum jackpot exceeds $99,638,178 the Powerball game has an average return to the player in excess of 100 percent (20,888,592 + 99,638,178 = 120,526,770).

Lotto South, Maryland Cash in Hand, Rhode Island Wild Money, Tri State Cash Lotto

These are examples of Pick Six, Pick Seven, Pick Five + LB, and Pick Four + Pick One, respectively. The calculations and analyses required here are so similar to the games in the examples above that I am going to leave these for you to do yourself. These games are described in chapter 2.

Nebraska Two by Two.

Nebraska's new MUSL game, Two by Two, is, not surprisingly, a Pick Four—Two by Two game. As indicated in chapter 2, the player picks two red numbers from 1 to 26, and two white numbers from 1 to 26. This gives the player four numbers altogether. The number of choices is obviously $\binom{26}{2}\binom{26}{2}$ or 105,625. The lottery also picks four numbers in this fashion. This partitions each 26-number set into two sets of two winners and 24 losers. Although the payoffs depend solely on the total number of matches, ignoring color, the computations require that color be considered. Here are the frequencies:

Match 2 Red & 2 White-	$\binom{2}{2}\binom{24}{0}\binom{2}{2}\binom{24}{0}$	=	1
Match 2 Red & 1 White-	$\binom{2}{2}\binom{24}{0}\binom{2}{1}\binom{24}{1}$	=	48
Match 1 Red & 2 White-	$\binom{2}{1}\binom{24}{1}\binom{2}{2}\binom{24}{0}$	=	48
Match 2 Red & 0 White-	$\binom{2}{2}\binom{24}{0}\binom{2}{0}\binom{24}{2}$	=	276
Match 1 Red & 1 White-	$\binom{2}{1}\binom{24}{1}\binom{2}{1}\binom{24}{1}$	=	2,304
Match 0 Red & 2 White-	$\binom{2}{0}\binom{24}{2}\binom{2}{2}\binom{24}{0}$	=	276
Match 1 Red & 0 White-	$\binom{2}{1}\binom{24}{1}\binom{2}{0}\binom{24}{2}$	=	13,248
Match 0 Red & 1 White-	$\binom{2}{0}\binom{24}{2}\binom{2}{1}\binom{24}{1}$	=	13,248
Match 0 Red & 0 White-	$\binom{2}{0}\binom{24}{2}\binom{2}{0}\binom{24}{2}$	=	76,176

Adding these results into groups of four, three, two, one, and zero matches, we can construct the return table in figure 8. The payoff for one match is a free play and the value of that, as we saw in the Missouri Show Me Five Paydown game, is simply the expected return to the player as a decimal. Since this is unknown we can just use the symbol x for it and proceed as we did in the Missouri game. Here is the table.

FIGURE 8

Nebraska Two by Two Return Table

OUTCOME	FREQUENCY	PAYOUT	PRODUCT
4 Matches	1	20,000	20,000
3 Matches	96	100	9,600
2 Matches	2,856	3	8,568
1 Match	26,496	x	26,496x
0 Matches	76,176	0	0
Total	105,625	—	38,168 + 26,496x

The overall expected return for the game can be calculated in the usual fashion as

$$\frac{38,168 + 26,496x}{105,625} = x \qquad (23)$$

which has the solution $x = 0.4824$. The house edge in this game is, therefore, 51.73 percent.

Louisiana Cash Quest

This game presents some challenges in the analysis department, but I think I can sort things out for you. To help with this sorting-out process I first want to quote from the Louisiana Lottery Web site, *www.lalottery.com:*

How to Play:

Each $1 play consists of 7 sets of four numbers. You choose one set of four numbers from 01 to 50 for the $50,000 top prize. Or use a quick pick to have your four numbers for the $50,000 prize randomly selected for you. The lottery terminal will randomly select an additional six sets of four numbers which are divided into separate prize groups on your ticket."

The key here is the word "randomly." I interpret this to mean that, though unlikely, all seven sets of four numbers could be identical. More likely is that some numbers could be repeated in more than one set, the frequency and density of occurrences depending solely upon probability. This contention is, I believe, further supported by the box in figure 9, which is copied directly from the Louisiana Lottery Web site.

FIGURE 9
Louisiana Cash Quest Web site Information

MATCH	WIN	ODDS
4 numbers from Group 1	$50,000*	1 in 230,300.00
4 numbers from one set in Group 2	$3,000	1 in 115,150.00
4 numbers from one set in Group 3	$500	1 in 57,575.00
3 numbers from one set in any group	$10	1 in 178.80
2 numbers from one set in any group	$1	1 in 5.30

Overall odds of winning a prize are approximately 1 in 5. The overall probabilities of winning a prize on a single $1 ticket include the possibility that some tickets may contain duplicate numbers and are based on the total number of possible combinations of tickets in the game.

* If more than 5 prizes are won in the $50,000 prize group in a single drawing, the top prize group becomes pari-mutuel on a total value of $250,000.

Notice that the statement after the prize structure indicates that repetitions of numbers may occur. The reason that I am being careful about this is that I want to treat each of the seven sets of four numbers as separate games, independent from each other, but having different pay structures. The plan is to calculate the expected return to the player for each set and then add the results. To reinforce this view I will refer to the choice of the four numbers in group 1 as *game 1*, the two sets of four in group 2 as *games 2 and 3*, and the four sets of four in group 3 as *games 4, 5, 6, and 7*. Since the four numbers in each game are selected from the numbers 1 through 50, there are $\binom{50}{4}$ or 230,300 sets of four number combinations possible in each game. This number will represent the total number of plays for each game. As usual we have to divide this total into the different salient outcomes for each game, namely, four matches, three matches, two matches, and one or no matches. Once the lottery picks its four numbers, the original number set of 1 through 50 is partitioned into four winners and 46 losers.

Here are the frequencies for each of the seven games:

Match 4	$\binom{4}{4}\binom{46}{0}$	=	1
Match 3	$\binom{4}{3}\binom{46}{1}$	=	184
Match 2	$\binom{4}{2}\binom{46}{2}$	=	6,210
Match 1	$\binom{4}{1}\binom{46}{3}$	=	60,720
Match 0	$\binom{4}{0}\binom{46}{4}$	=	163,185
		Total =	230,300

Notice that the losing frequency is the sum of the last two numbers in this list and is 223,905. With these numbers in hand we can construct the following table:

FIGURE 10
Louisiana Cash Quest Returns per Game

OUTCOME	FREQUENCY	G1	PROD.	G2–G3	PROD.	G4–G7	PROD.
Match 4	1	50,000	50,000	3,000	3,000	500	500
Match 3	184	10	1,840	10	1,840	10	1,840
Match 2	6,210	1	6,210	1	6,210	1	6,210
Losers	223,905	0	0	0	0	0	0
Total	230,300	—	58,050	—	11,050	—	8,550

Now here is the overview. For our one-dollar wager on this game we get to play seven independent games. The frequencies are the same for each game and the pay structure for each game is given in figure 10 under the columns G1, G2–G3, and G4–G7. Using this data, figure 10 gives us the return for each of the games. If we play Cash Quest 230,300 times for one dollar, game 1 will return 58,050 to us, games 2 and 3 will each return 11,050, and games 4, 5, 6, and 7 will each return 8,550 to us. Adding these up we have:

$$1 \cdot 58{,}050 + 2 \cdot 11{,}050 + 4 \cdot 8{,}550 = 114{,}350 \quad (24)$$

If we divide this figure by 230,300 we get the fractional return to the player. It is 0.496526 or approximately 49.65 percent. The house edge is, therefore, 50.35 percent.

Before I leave this game I want to comment on the figures given under the column "Odds" in figure 9. The first figure is exactly right and the next two are close enough. The last two are a bit off. It's no big deal but is mathematically interesting, so let me show you what I mean. I'll address the last row, which reads, "2 numbers from any one set in any group." I take this to mean that if exactly two numbers match in at least one set then the player wins one dollar for that set; the player could match exactly two in more than one set and win one dollar for each such match. This is the most generous interpretation of the game and is consistent with the information provided by the lottery.

One must be careful when trying to calculate the chances of getting at least one pair match in the seven sets. A common error is to add probabilities over events that have outcomes in common and thereby count some outcomes more than once. For example, if one added the probability of getting a pair in group 2 and anything else in the other groups and the probability of a pair in group 3 and anything else in the other groups, the probability of getting a pair in both groups would be added twice. In Louisiana Cash Quest this error would occur if one simply divides seven times 6,210 into 230,300; the result is 5.2979 or approximately 5.30. This number makes the probability of success appear larger than it really is. A slick way to avoid that error, specifically in the problem at hand, is to first compute the probability of not making an exact two-number match in a single set. Since there are 230,300 possible choices for the player's numbers and 6,210 of these will exactly match two of the lottery's numbers, there are 230,300—6,210 or 224,090 ways to not make exact pair matches. Hence the probability of not making a pair match in any particular set is $\frac{224,090}{230,300}$ or 0.973035171. Since each set is independent from the other, the probability of not making a pair match in any of the seven sets is $(0.973035171)^7$ or 0.825847332. The probability of making at least one pair match is 1 minus the probability of not making any pair match, that is, 1 − 0.825847332 or 0.173152667. The reciprocal of this number is the chance of making at least one exact pair match in the seven sets; it is one in 5.74. This figure says nothing about the other possibilities that could occur, only that there is at least one exact pair match. Using the same type of calculation, the chance of making at least one exact triple match in the seven sets is one in 179.23. Note that under the most generous interpretation for the player, both of these numbers represent probabilities that are slightly smaller than one would infer from the numbers stated by the Louisiana Lottery. To be fair to the lottery, though, ignoring common outcomes in lottery calculations is a common practice since the probabilities are so tiny, but in this case it did make a slight difference.

The calculation in the previous paragraph can be used to easily obtain the overall chances that the player will win something (counting one dollar as a "win"). In each game the chance of winning something is 6,395 out of 230,300 so the chance of winning nothing is 230,300 − 6,395 or 223,905. The probability of winning nothing in a particular game is, therefore, $^{223,905}/_{230,300}$ or 0.972231871. Thus, the probability of winning nothing in all seven games is $(0.972231871)^7$ or 0.821086624. The probability of winning something is 1 − 0.821086624 or 0.178913375. This represents an overall chance of approximately 1 in 5.589 of winning something.

Winner Wonderland

Christmas Day at the Catlins' is like Christmas Day in homes across the country. It is a joyous, boisterous, noisy frenzy of wrapping paper, presents, laughter, grandchildren, and too much food. With my wife, Mary, our two children and their spouses, our four grandchildren, and their Aunt Linda, we inevitably have 11 folks packed in our little house, and it is a wonderful time. We prepare a big brunch of juice, coffee, tea, lox, bagels, bacon, coffeecakes, fruit, and a big cheese soufflé. Although Mary pitches in and does a lot of the work preparing this feast, I am the cook in our household. Christmas morning invariably finds me attending to last-minute details, especially timing that soufflé, while the guests are patiently waiting to eat. The kids, of course, can be kept occupied by opening a couple of presents, but what of the adults?

My solution to this lull is to buy state lottery scratch tickets and let each adult (including myself!) pick two of them. Every Christmas/Hanukkah season the Massachusetts State Lottery issues special scratch tickets in two-dollar and five-dollar denominations; in 2001 the five-dollar scratch ticket was called Winner Wonderland. You can see what it looks like in figure 11. This scratch ticket game is very similar to hundreds of other scratch tickets games operated by every lottery in the nation. Everyone looks forward to this annual ritual and we have a lot of fun with it. The total return for the collective Catlin family hasn't been bad either, averaging around 75 percent for the last four years. Of course, that figure got a big boost two years ago, when my son-in-law Larry hit ten $10 winners for a total of $100. As far back as I can remember, yours truly hasn't won a dime. However, you'll note that the ticket in figure 11 hasn't been scratched. I think I'll wait until this book is finished to scratch that ticket;

it will give me an incentive to keep writing—and, who knows, I might hit the big one!

FIGURE 11
Winner Wonderland Scratch Ticket

There is no probability at work in scratch tickets. The frequencies are determined before the tickets are printed and if all of the tickets of a particular kind are sold then the frequency of each winning (or losing) combination will be exactly as planned. In figure 12 I have listed the various winning combinations and their frequencies for the Winner Wonderland ticket. The number of tickets issued, and hopefully sold, was 25,200,000. This represents total receipts of $126,000,000. Of these, as you can see from figure 12, $90,410,000 is returned to the players, which represents a 71.75 percent return. The house edge is, therefore, 28.25 percent. This looks small relative to other lottery games. Remember, though—like Keno, this is a game of instant winners. I have observed that, when players win the price of the ticket, five dollars in this case, they frequently use the money to purchase another ticket, most likely a loser. This is known as *churning*. The same phenomenon happens in Keno. The more that small winners are churned the less money is kept by the players and the better it is for the lottery. The average return for the Keno game is approximately 70 percent, depending upon how many spots you play, so the 28.25 percent figure is consistent with this. Lest you suspect that in Massachusetts the cheaper scratch tickets extract a larger percentage from the players, I checked a one-dollar game called Quick Cash and found that the return to players was 69.99 percent, again right around the 30 percent house edge figure. Finally, I checked three more games, to find that they were all in the 70 percent return neighborhood. This is consistent with the Massachusetts State Lottery's information.

I am not privy to detailed data about the structure of scratch tickets in all other states, but 35 of them did respond to my requests for information about their scratch tickets. On the basis of these responses I can tell you that scratch tickets have an expected return to the player of approximately 57 percent to 76 percent with most returns in the mid-60s. Some states, like Massachusetts, seem to use almost the same return for all tickets and others, like Maryland, return more to higher-denomination tickets. See the appendix for details.

FIGURE 12

Winner Wonderland Returns

OUTCOME	FREQUENCY	PAYOUT	PRODUCT
1 $250,000 Hit	25	250,000	6,250,000
10 $500 Hits (Snowflake)	525	5,000	2,625,000
10 $500 Hits	325	5,000	1,635,000
1 $5,000 Hit	350	5,000	1,635,000
10 $100 Hits (Snowflake)	700	1,000	700,000
10 $100 Hits	700	1,000	700,000
5 $200 Hits	700	1,000	700,000
1 $1,000 Hit	350	1,000	350,000
10 $50 Hits (Snowflake)	2,625	500	1,312,500
10 $50 Hits	2,625	500	1,312,500
6 $50 and 2 $100 Hits	2,625	500	1,312,500
5 $100 Hits	2,625	500	1,312,500
1 $500 Hit	1,750	500	875,000
10 $40 Hits (Snowflake)	3,500	400	1,400,000
10 $40 Hits	3,500	400	1,400,000
8 $50 Hits	3,500	400	1,400,000
4 $100 Hits	2,625	400	1,050,000
1 $400 Hit	2,625	400	1,050,000
10 $20 Hits (Snowflake)	7,875	200	1,575,000
10 $20 Hits	7,875	200	1,575,000
5 $20 and 2 $50 Hits	7,000	200	1,400,000
4 $50 Hits	6,300	200	1,260,000

FIGURE 12 (CONTINUED)

OUTCOME	FREQUENCY	PAYOUT	PRODUCT
1 $200 Hit	6,300	200	1,260,000
10 $10 Hits (Snowflake)	16,800	100	1,680,000
10 $10 Hits *[Larry!]*	16,800	100	1,680,000
5 $20 Hits	16,800	100	1,680,000
2 $50 Hits	16,800	100	1,680,000
1 $100 Hit	16,800	100	1,680,000
10 $5 Hits (Snowflake)	16,800	50	840,000
10 $5 Hits	16,800	50	840,000
8 $5 Hits and 1 $10 Hit	16,800	50	840,000
5 $10 Hits	16,800	50	840,000
1 $50 Hit	16,800	50	840,000
8 $5 Hits	50,400	40	2,016,000
4 $10 Hits	50,400	40	2,016,000
2 $20 Hits	33,600	40	1,344,000
1 $40 Hit	33,600	40	1,344,000
10 $2 Hits (Snowflake)	100,800	20	1,016,000
5 $2 and 2 $5 Hits	100,800	20	1,016,000
4 $5 Hits	100,800	20	1,016,000
2 $10 Hits	100,800	20	1,016,000
1 $20 Hit	100,800	20	1,016,000
5 $2 Hits	672,000	10	6,720,000
2 $5 Hits	672,000	10	6,720,000
1 $10 Hit	672,000	10	6,720,000
1 $5 Hit	2,352,000	5	11,760,000
Losers	19,925,000	0	0
Total	25,200,000	—	90,410,000

City Picks of Wisconsin

The game of City Picks offered by the Wisconsin State Lottery was, from an analysis point of view, the most interesting game that I encountered in any state lottery. The determination of its house edge required a piece of mathematics called a derangement that goes back to the Swiss mathematician Leonhard Euler (1707–83). Let me illustrate the idea with an example.

Suppose we consider the numbers 1, 2, 3, and 4 in that order. We already know what a permutation of these numbers is; it is simply a rearrangement of them into a different order, and we know that there are 4! or 24 such permutations. Suppose now that we add a stipulation that, when rearranging these numbers, no number is to occupy the spot that it did prior to the rearrangement. A permutation with this added stipulation is called a *derangement*. In the example at hand there are nine possible derangements. They are:

2 3 4 1	3 4 2 1	2 1 4 3
2 4 1 3	4 1 2 3	3 1 4 2
3 4 1 2	4 3 1 2	4 3 2 1

The problem we want to solve is this. Given n integers 1 2 3 . . . n, how many of the $n!$ permutations are derangements? If you think about this it is a tough problem.

Denoting the number of derangements of n integers by d_n, Euler gave a recursive formula for this number. Clearly $d_1 = 0$ and $d_2 = 1$. Euler's formula is:

$$d_n = (n - 1)(d_{n-1} + d_{n-2})$$ (25)

I am not going to try and prove to you that it is correct but I would like to show you how to use the formula. Letting $n = 3$ in (25) we have

$$d_3 = (3 - 1)(d_2 + d_1) = 2(1 + 0) = 2 \qquad (26)$$

Now that we have d_3 we can use it and d_2 to calculate d_4:

$$d_4 = (4 - 1)(d_3 + d_2) = 3(2 + 1) = 9 \qquad (27)$$

See, this is what we discovered in our example above. Continuing in this fashion we can construct the following table:

FIGURE 13
Number of Derangements

n	d_n
1	0
2	1
3	2
4	9
5	44
6	265
7	1,854
8	14,933
9	133,496

The information in figure 13 is everything we need to analyze the City Picks game. Here is the game.

A City Picks card lists nine Wisconsin cities. They are:

Chippewa Falls	Milwaukee
Dodgeville	Superior
Green Bay	Two Rivers
Kenosha	Wisconsin Rapids
Madison	

The player then puts these cities in a personal order, one through nine. The lottery randomly does the same. The player's prize is determined by how many matches occur, that is, how many times the player and the lottery have the same city in the same position. I'll give the pay table below. An example is helpful here. Suppose that the player puts the cities in alphabetical order as above. Here are the player's and the lottery's order:

Player's Order	Lottery's Order
Chippewa Falls	Dodgeville
Dodgeville	Superior
Green Bay	Green Bay
Kenosha	Madison
Madison	Superior
Milwaukee	Milwaukee
Superior	Wisconsin Rapids
Two Rivers	Two Rivers
Wisconsin Rapids	Kenosha

Note that there are three matches: Green Bay, Milwaukee, and Two Rivers.

Here comes the mathematics. We know that there are 9! or 362,880 ways the player can arrange the nine cities in order. Only one of these matches the lottery's ordering. How many ways can we get eight matches? None! If we have eight perfect matches then there is only one city left, so that has to match as well. What about other numbers? Let's take a look at, say, five. Now there are $\binom{9}{5}$ different ways that five of the player's picks can match the lottery's picks. So far, so good. For each of these choices the four remaining numbers have to not match the lottery's picks. That's right, they have to be a *derangement* of the lottery's four picks. So the number of ways to have five matches in this game is $\binom{9}{5}d_4$ or $126 \cdot 9$, which is 1,134. I think you can see that the general formula for the number of matches in the City Picks game is given by

$$\text{Number of k matches} = \binom{9}{k}d_{9-k} \qquad (28)$$

Here is the payoff and frequency table for the City Picks game:

FIGURE 14
City Picks House Edge Table

OUTCOME	FREQUENCY	PAYOUT	PRODUCT
9 Matches	1	50,000	50,000
7 Matches	36	1,000	36,000
6 Matches	168	200	33,600
5 Matches	1,134	20	22,680
4 Matches	5,544	4	22,176
3 Matches	22,260	1	22,260
2 Matches	66,744	0	0
1 Match	133,497	0	0
0 Matches	133,496	0	0
Total	362,880	—	186,716

The return to the player in the City Picks game is $186,700/362,880$ or approximately 0.51454. We'll call this 51.5 percent, so the house edge is 48.5 percent.

Nevada Numbers

In a sense, a discussion of this game doesn't belong in this book since it is not a state lottery, however, I am including it because I think it is interesting to see the effect that the Primm phenomenon is having on Las Vegas. Nevada Numbers is a game that is run by Park Place Entertainment.[*] It is currently available at the Keno booths in Bally's Las Vegas, Flamingo Las Vegas, Las Vegas Hilton, Flamingo Laughlin, Paris Las Vegas, and Reno Hilton. It was clearly a cheap game to implement since it uses the existing 80 Keno numbers and did not require new equipment.

Nevada Numbers is essentially a five-spot Keno ticket with a jackpot rollover feature. There are $\binom{80}{5}$ = 24,040,016 different ways to pick five numbers from 80. After the lottery picks its five numbers in its daily drawing, the 80 numbers are partitioned into two sets consisting of five winners and 75 losers. The frequency of matches is the usual type of calculation that we have been doing:

5 Matches	$\binom{5}{5}\binom{75}{0}$	=	1
4 Matches	$\binom{5}{4}\binom{75}{1}$	=	375
3 Matches	$\binom{5}{3}\binom{75}{2}$	=	27,750
2 Matches	$\binom{5}{2}\binom{75}{3}$	=	675,250
1 Match	$\binom{5}{1}\binom{75}{4}$	=	6,077,250
0 Matches	$\binom{5}{0}\binom{75}{5}$	=	17,259,390
		Total =	24,040,016

[*] It sure wouldn't be run by the owners of the Primm Valley Lotto Store, MGM-Mirage.

The game costs two dollars to play. The progressive jackpot starts at five million dollars and, according to Nevada
Numbers, increases with each ticket sold. Figure 15 shows
the payoff structure, and the return for Nevada Numbers assuming the game is played 24,040,016 times and everything
happens as probability theory predicts. Since tickets cost the
player two dollars each, this represents a total investment
of $48,080,032.00. If the jackpot is five million dollars annu-
itized over 20 payments, a jackpot pool of $3,271,330 is re-
quired to fund the prize (see the following section on annuities). There is no information available concerning the
growth rate of the jackpot. The fixed payouts represent 18
percent of the handle. A jackpot of $15,307,266 plus non-
jackpot payments of $8,732,750 total $24,050,016, which
would represent an average payback to the player of 50 percent assuming 24,040,016 in sales. Assuming this is the typical return the lottery seeks, the jackpot would have to grow
from zero to $15,307,266 in 24,040,016 sales. The increment
per ticket sold, therefore, would be about 64¢ per sale or 32
percent of the receipts. Using this figure, 5,111,453 sales
would have to occur before the minimum jackpot could be
covered. After that the 64¢/36¢ contribution to jackpot/non-
jackpot pools would insure a 50 percent house edge. Understand that the 64¢ increment is simply my best guess based
on the assumptions and the analysis above; I have no hard
data from the Nevada Numbers game. Note that whenever
the lump sum jackpot exceeds $39,347,282 the game returns
an average of over 100 percent to the players.

FIGURE 15
Return Table for Nevada Numbers

OUTCOME	FREQUENCY	PAYOUT	PRODUCT
5 Matches	1	Jackpot	JP
4 Matches	375	2,000	750,000
3 Matches	27,750	20	555,000
2 Matches	675,250	2	1,350,500
1 Match	6,077,250	1	6,077,250
0 Matches	17,259,390	0	0
Total	24,040,016	—	JP + 8,732,750

So will Park Place Entertainment and their Nevada Numbers game stem the tide of Las Vegas residents to the Primm Valley Lotto Store? It's not that easy to place a wager on the Nevada Numbers game since you have to place it at a Keno outlet in one of their properties. On the other hand, it is easier (and probably cheaper) than driving to Primm. On average, however, the California Super Lotto Plus Jackpot will be larger than that of the Nevada Numbers game. Here's another question to consider: if Nevada Numbers catches on will we see Mississippi Millions or Gold Coast Gold? Time will tell.

Annuities Versus Lump Sums

All games that offer large, progressive, jackpots pay the jackpots in installments, a form of payment that is a type of *annuity*. Usually the number of payments is either 20, 25, or 30 and they are paid annually, which means that the period over which the annuity runs is 19, 24, or 29 years respectively. In most, if not all, venues, players have the option of receiving a one-lump-sum payment, which is usually considerably less than the jackpot figure. The lump sum is the amount of money that the lottery would have to invest and draw on annually in order to meet its obligations to pay the annuity. The effects of inflation and other economic fluctuations are ignored in coming up with this figure. The formula for determining this annuity pool is rather complicated to derive, so I am not going to do it here, but I will report the end result. It is:

$$\textit{Annuity Pool for n Payments} = \left[\frac{(1+r)^{n-1}-1}{r(1+r)^{n-1}}+1\right]\frac{Prize}{n} \quad (29)$$

where r is the interest rate as a decimal that one could expect over the life of the pool. Currently CDs pay around two percent and corporate bonds or preferred stocks can be found that pay around seven percent so I'll use five percent as a reasonable rate of return.[*] With this assumption the formula in (29) becomes

$$\textit{Annuity Pool for n Payments} = \left[\frac{(1.05)^{n-1}-1}{(.05)(1.05)^{n}}+1\right]\frac{Prize}{n} \quad (30)$$

Evaluating (30) for $n = 20$ and 25 respectively we obtain

$$\textit{Annuity Pool for 20 payments} = 0.654266043 \cdot \textit{Prize} \quad (31)$$

and

$$\textit{Annuity Pool for 25 payments} = 0.591945671 \cdot \textit{Prize} \quad (32)$$

---

[*] Lotteries typically use U.S. Treasury bonds and form a bond ladder. A bond ladder is a mixture of short, medium, and long term bonds that mature at staggered time intervals.

In other words, if the jackpot prize was $1,000,000 the lottery could invest $591,945.68* at five percent annually and pay the winner 25 annual payments of $40,000. This is what the prize as an annuity is worth, so it is also what the prize as a lump sum is worth.

Now one interesting thing is that some lotteries simply pay the winner a lump sum of half the jackpot and claim to put their additional profit from this transaction into other prizes. I'm sure they do. Most, such as MUSL, simply give winners the amount in the prize pool at the time of the win.

Pari-mutuel Payments

Pari-mutuel wagering in the United States is found in horse racing, dog racing, and Jai Alai. The name "pari-mutuel" is a contraction of "Paris mutuel"; the system was invented in Paris, France, in 1865 by Pierre Oller. The idea is quite simple. Let's look at an example by seeing how payoffs for a Show wager are determined in a horse race.

A Show wager on a particular horse is a bet that the horse will come in either first, second, or third (Win, Place, Show). Once the race has been run the operators of the track take all of the Show wagers on the race and lump them together in a pool. The track then extracts its cut, usually 15 percent of the pool, and the remaining money is used to pay Show bets on the three first-place horses. This remaining money is divided equally into three pools, each one used to pay the

---

* You always round up to the next penny to be assured that the pool has sufficient funds.

Show wagers on one of the three horses finishing in the money. For example, the number of Show wagers on the winning horse is divided into the amount of money in the winning horse's pool and that is the amount paid to each such wager. Same for second- and third-place finishers. That's it.*

Many state lotteries advertise that their prizes are pari-mutuel. If they truly were then each prize level would have same amount of money in its payout pool. As we will see this is definitely not the case with state lotteries. To illustrate a typical state lottery pari-mutuel scheme I'll use the Super Six Lotto game from the Pennsylvania State Lottery. I found this lottery to have the clearest and easiest-to-find description of its payoff procedure.

The Super Six Lotto game is a Pick Six from 69–type game. Each player receives three games for one dollar so the cost per game is 33⅓¢. The player gets to pick the six numbers for one of the games but the next two games must be computer-generated quick picks. This ensures that the three six-number sets are independent so the situation is equivalent to each player playing three independent games. Now

---

* It is actually a bit more complicated than this. Since betting windows don't want to deal with pennies, the procedure is as follows. After the original 15% has been deducted, the total amount of Show wagers on the first three horses is temporarily removed from the pool and the remainder is divided into three equal parts for each of the three horses in the money. The number of wagers on each horse is divided into that horse's pool and the result is rounded down to the nearest nickel (or sometimes dime). This is called *breakage,* and the extra money is kept by the track. The cost of the original ticket is added to the rounded number and that is the payoff on that horse.

$\binom{69}{6}$ = 119,877,472, so let's suppose that this many people play the game. The total revenue is then $119,877,472. The lottery sets aside 52 percent of this, or $62,336,285, as a prize pool. The lottery then assigns 76 percent of this to the jackpot prize pool, 8 percent to the second prize pool, 7.5 percent to the third prize pool, and 8.5 percent to the fourth place pool. Given this, we can create the table in figure 16. Notice that the frequency total of 359,632,416 is exactly three times 119,877,472, the number of players. That is because each player gets three chances at prizes. I should point out that the analysis could have been done using one game at a cost of 33⅓¢—the figures in the last column of figure 16 would have been exactly the same.

FIGURE 16
Average Pari-mutuel Payouts for Super Six Lotto

OUTCOME	FREQUENCY	PAYOUT	PAYOUT/FREQ.
6 Matches	3	47,375,577	15,791,853.00
5 Matches	1,134	4,986,903	4,397.62
4 Matches	87,885	4,675,221	54.20
3 Matches	2,382,660	5,298,584	2.22
Losers	357,160,734	0	0.00
Total	359,632,416	62,336,285	—

It should be pointed out that, although the typical average payout for the jackpot is $15,791,859, by structuring the game as it has the lottery can advertise jackpots three times as large. This brings up another issue. How big should the jackpot be for a break-even game? Well, the total sales are

$119,877,472 and the non-jackpot payouts are $14,960,708, so the difference is $104,916,764. Of course one would either have to be the sole jackpot winner or win all three games to receive this amount. Tough! You can think of the same person playing all of the 119,877,472 combinations three times each and with the above lump-sum jackpot that person would break even.

Notice that the percentage of the prize pool dedicated to jackpots is over three times as large as that dedicated to the other prizes. This is typical of many state lotteries, even those with fixed non-jackpot prizes. I suspect that the reason is twofold. First, larger advertised jackpots create more revenue. Second, there is generally a guaranteed minimum for the jackpot (three million dollars in the case of Pennsylvania), so the lottery wants the actual jackpot pool to exceed this number as quickly as possible.

Some Afterthoughts

The calculations I did above should cover most lottery games that you might encounter. If you find a game that interests you, find its classification in chapter 2 and follow the example in this chapter for a game of that type. In case the game does not fit into one of my classifications, you still may find enough mathematical material in this chapter to devise an analysis. If you're stumped you can reach me through the Web site *www.scoblete.com* and I will be glad to help you.

From the above examples, and the information in the appendix, we can draw some general conclusions. The typical return to the player in most lottery games is right around 50 percent. For most Keno and scratch tickets the return is somewhere in the vicinity of 60 percent to 70 percent.

One of the unusual results above was the large house edge in the Missouri Show Me Paydown game when a jackpot occurs. This game can afford a much larger jackpot, but I'll leave it to you to figure out how much larger. The now-defunct Rolldown game that was offered by MUSL used to roll down the jackpot in a pari-mutuel fashion—29.5 percent to the four match winners, 28.5 percent to the three match winners, and 42 percent to the two match winners. This meant that the percentage payouts in the jackpot and non-jackpot games were identical.

As we saw above, games with progressive jackpots sometimes turn positive. The point at which this happens is generally easy to determine unless the payout schedule is pari-mutuel. The relevant examples in this chapter show you how this figure can be calculated. When the pay schedule is pari-mutuel one needs to know the prize pool percentages, and the jackpot/non-jackpot mix. Sometimes this information is readily available and sometimes it is not. For the games in existence as of this writing, I have listed break even numbers, as near as I could determine them, in the appendix. In chapter 5 I'll have more comments on these break-even points. The appendix also lists the house edge for games that do not have progressive jackpots. Again, if the prize structure is pari-mutuel then the return to the player is simply the prize pool percentage of the total sales. Sometimes this figure was clearly stated by the individual lottery, sometimes the lottery conveyed the information to me, and sometimes I had to estimate it.

I should mention that all of the information in the appendix is subject to change, as lotteries constantly refine their games. This is one of the reasons that I showed you how to analyze the games; if they change you can do the analysis yourself. As I was writing this section an article appeared in our local paper, the *Daily Hampshire Gazette*, entitled "State Looks to Smaller Lottery Prizes." The article describes how Massachusetts state legislators are currently arguing over whether or not to cut percentage returns on lottery games. Such a move might well decrease rather than increase revenue. My own opinion is that lowering the house edge on instant games, such as scratch tickets and Keno, by increasing the smaller prizes might actually boost revenues due to the previously mentioned churning effect. (I would be interested to see a statistical study determining the instant-game prize mix that produces the most revenue.). In any event, by the time you read this it may well be the case that the figures for Massachusetts stated in the appendix are out of date. This may be true of certain other states as well. When it comes to gambling, I'm not sure that legislators know what they're doing.*

We began our study of state lotteries back in chapter 1 by focusing on the Primm Valley Lotto Store and the California Super Lotto Plus game in California. I mentioned then that the chance of winning the big prize is minuscule. Now it is easy to support such an assertion. After slogging through this

---

* For an excellent article about this very topic, see John Robison's article "Politicians See Gaming Taxes as Easy Money," which appeared July 19, 2002, on *www.scoblete.com*.

last chapter you well know that the number of possible combinations in Super Lotto Plus is $\binom{47}{5}\binom{27}{1}$, which is 41,416,353. Mr. Castellano, the June 23, 2001, winner, had overcome chances of 1 in 41,416,353 when he came up with the winning ticket. In the next chapter we'll meet some other lucky folks—and some not so lucky. For now, to paraphrase the monsignor, "Go in peace; the math is ended."

4

Lottery Luck: The Good, the Bad, and the Ugly

Luck

It is interesting to think back and recall lucky and unlucky events in one's life. No doubt you've had your share of each. I don't mean the usual stuff that most everyone can claim—being born, getting married, and losing parents. I mean bolt-out-of-the-blue events that, while not earth-shattering, did leave an impression of luckiness or unluckiness on your memory. For me, the unlucky events were: breaking a collar bone when I was a child, a ski accident that I still feel to this day, and, most recently, getting an attack of appendicitis on a Saturday night when the hospital emergency room was especially busy. On the lucky side of the coin, though, there was one night in Las Vegas that beat all my other good-luck memories. A big win? No, better than that.

Several years ago I flew in to McCarran Field in Las Vegas for a few days at Caesars Palace. I had reserved a car at one of the many car rental agencies that ring the airport. This one was located right on Swenson Street, at that time the main one-way street out of the airport. On my arrival I was told that I was being bumped up a grade, and that I would have a four-door rather than my usual two-door "el cheapo" car. Fine. I put the contract in my canvas briefcase and followed the directions to my car. When I got to the vehicle identified as my car I immediately noticed that it was a two-door. Not wanting to take the wrong car I put my briefcase on the top of the car, fished out the contract, checked the VIN number, and noticed that the number on the contract didn't match that of the auto. So I went back to the office and told them of my concern.

The office confirmed the mix-up and drew up a new contract that did match my vehicle, and away I went down Swenson Street wondering what sort of exotic room at Caesars awaited me this time. During my previous trip I had a room that included a circular bed, a spa right in the bedroom, and a mirror over the bed. As I told one of my friends, "It looked as if the room had been designed by two hookers and a pit boss."

These musings were suddenly interrupted. Had I put my briefcase back in the car? Gulp! In my briefcase were my plane tickets, my airport parking receipt, my checkbook, my room reservation confirmation, all my player's cards, and two thousand dollars in cash. I pulled to the Swenson Street curb, looked in the back seat, searched the trunk, and checked the roof of the car. No briefcase!

I stood there dazed. "Well," I thought, "I'll have to take Tropicana to Paradise, circle back around to the beginning of Swenson Street, and hope that by the time I get there my briefcase will either still be in the rental agency's parking lot or lying somewhere on the street." I was in panic mode. As I was about to lower the trunk lid a car pulled up next to me and the driver yelled out of his window, "Hey, is your name Catlin?" Startled, I replied "yes," whereupon he tossed my briefcase to me, and before I could even say "thanks" he was gone like a shot. I would have cheerfully handed the guy a hundred-dollar bill. Although this guy had gone through my briefcase in order to identify me, everything was there—including the two thousand dollars.

When I finally got settled in at Caesars and sat down at a blackjack table, the dealer beat me out of five hundred dollars during the first 20 minutes of play. The dealer just shook his head. "Not your lucky day, I guess."

"No," I replied, "this is one of the luckiest days of my life." I'm sure he thought I was nuts.

The Good

I wish that I could report to you that I have had firsthand experience at winning lotteries, but my record in that department is abysmal. I have, however, personally known a couple of lottery winners. One was Cyndy, a secretary in the Department of Mathematics and Statistics at the University of Massachusetts, Amherst, where I have been a professor for the past 37 years. Cyndy hit a scratch ticket for $50,000 and it couldn't have happened to a nicer person. She was a good worker and had a terrific sense of humor; I'm happy that she won. The other winner was a student of mine. Here's his story.

In the early '80s I was teaching a course in linear algebra. One of my students hit one of the Massachusetts Lottery's games—I think it was Megabucks—for around $180,000. Here's the interesting part: In those days the lottery here used to have promotions that included two-for-one plays, discounts on scratch tickets, and sometimes free plays. My student had received one of these free plays in the mail. He had never played the lottery in his life and had purchased just one ticket with his free play. That ticket, along with four others, hit the big prize (which is why his prize wasn't in the million-dollar vicinity). I don't remember his name, which is probably okay with him, but I do remember that he was a good student and a pleasant fellow. And, no, he didn't quit school and travel to Europe; he was with me for the entire semester.

There are hundreds of other lottery winners all across this country, none of whom I know. Often they are just ordinary folks like the two I mentioned above. Take Edward Gralinski, for example. Mr. Gralinski is a farmer in the town of Hadley, Massachusetts, which is right next to my own town of Amherst. During the last week of May 2002, he bought a Casino Nights scratch ticket and scratched off a one-million-dollar winner. He bought the ticket at O'Connell's Convenience Plus gas station on Route 9, the owner of which received $10,000 for selling the ticket. After deducting taxes,

Gralinski will receive $34,000 annually for 20 years. What are his plans? He plans to keep working the farm and says the money will help since the farm has been going through some bad years.

Mr. Gralinski's story is reminiscent of that of Albert Knights of Maine, who won a $5.9 million jackpot. Did he retire? No, he returned to his $160-a-week position as a garbage man. When interviewed by *People* magazine he simply said, "I wasn't ready to retire. Besides, [my job] keeps me out of mischief and from fightin' with the old lady."

When Harold St. Pierre of Lake Charles, Louisiana, won one million dollars in the Louisiana Lotto game in August of 2001, he was not quite as blasé as Mr. Knights. However, it was clear that he and his wife Liz were going to be the same folks that they always were—with a couple of changes. Liz had always wanted to own a vintage 1967 Ford Mustang and Harold wanted a new fishing boat. Harold says that he planned to buy Liz the Mustang, then buy the fishing boat, and then take a trip. After that, deducting state and federal taxes, there was about $650,000, which was simply to be put into savings. St. Pierre, who works in the maintenance department at the Lake Charles Citgo refinery, says that he usually buys a Lotto ticket and a Powerball ticket every week. When he appeared at the Louisiana Lottery Corporation headquarters in Baton Rouge on August 16 he said, "I knew I won something, but I wasn't sure how much. I called family members to find out the jackpot amount, but no one knew it. I certainly didn't think I won a million dollars." A vintage Mustang, a good fishing boat, and money in the bank—sounds like a good life to me.

The dollar amounts in the stories above are certainly not chump change to the folks who won them, but in the world of super lotteries they might be considered as such. Consider this story. Maria Grasso, a Chilean woman living in the United States, was a babysitter for a millionaire and is now is a millionaire herself—several times over. On April 6, 1999, she overcame chances of 76-million-to-one to win the Big Game jackpot of almost two hundred million dollars. At the time it was the biggest lottery prize won by a single person.

The 54-year-old Ms. Grasso had come to the United States from Chile 28 years ago and had been working in Boston as a nanny to four children. She became a U.S. citizen in 1984. She said she was not sure what she would do with the money. "I couldn't believe it. I haven't had time to think clearly." Nevertheless, she did say that her priority now was to help her own two children and the rest of her family, most of them currently living in Chile. Her employer said, "She's the kind of person who deserves a good turn in life," and, after winning, she resigned her position. In Chile, her sister Ana was quoted as saying, "She fully deserves what has happened to her. She worked hard all her life to help her family, especially our mother."

When Larry Ross, a swimming pool installer from Shelby Township, Michigan, came forward in early May of 2000 to collect $181 million, his half of the Big Game jackpot, he could have yelled "Hot diggity dog!" Ross, 47, had stopped at Mr. K's Party Shoppe in Utica, Michigan, to buy himself a hot dog. Unfortunately—or fortunately, as it turned out—the smallest bill he had was one hundred dollars. Since his wife, Nancy, had asked him to buy some lottery tickets, he paid for his hot dog with the hundred dollars and took his change in lottery tickets, 98 of them. One of the tickets had the winning numbers 33, 2, 1, 12, 37, and the Big Money Ball 4. Ross, the owner of Bush Pools, was interviewed by Brian Dickerson of the *Detroit Free Press* a couple of years after his win; though the Rosses have moved up to a larger home, they still live in the same school district as before. Ross explained that staying put was a no-brainer. His daughter still had four years of high school left when their win occurred, and he and Nancy were determined not to uproot her. Although the Rosses now own a yacht and a vacation home in Arizona, they don't anticipate leaving Shelby Township even after their daughter graduates. "This is home," Ross said, "and unless something freaky happens, we're not going anywhere."

One of the first people Ross called after he won was Gary Aidem, an ex-IRS agent who had helped Ross's widowed mother-in-law with her investments several years earlier. Under Aidem's advice Ross's assets are distributed among five banks, two brokerage houses, and a real estate investment fund. Today Aidem works full-time overseeing the bankers and investment brokers who manage the Ross fortune. It is interesting to note that Ross has allocated just five percent of his portfolio to the stock market. Aidem says that if he had agreed to the 30 percent allocation that several money managers suggested "he'd be out $12 to $15 million by now."

Dickerson asked Ross about any advice he could give to potential winners. "He seemed relieved to learn all I wanted was advice," Dickerson said. According to Ross, "About 50 percent of the phone calls I get these days are along the lines of, 'Can I see you about something later?' And you know what *that* means."

On Tuesday, April 16, 2002, Erika Greene, a 20-year-old warehouse worker in the state of Georgia, spent all the money she was carrying, $10, to buy 10 lottery tickets. The transaction took place at a Texaco station in Dacula, a small town in north Georgia about two miles from Erika's home. She picked one number set and let the computer pick the other nine. The game was the Big Game, the same game that was won by Maria Grasso and Larry Ross. There had been no jackpot winners since early February and the jackpot stood at $331 million.

Some two hours later the Big Game drawing took place and the winning combination was 7, 10, 25, 26, 27, and bonus number 23. This exact combination was on one of Erika's computer-generated tickets. "I said, 'I know I'm see-ing this wrong. It's got to be wrong,'" Greene said. But her mother confirmed that the winning number was indeed on one of her tickets. The first person Erika called after discov-ering her win was her boyfriend, Mike Swofford. "I think I said, 'Baby, I won!'"

Erika's ticket was one of three winning tickets purchased for the drawing and was worth $110,333,333. The other two winning tickets were sold in Illinois and New Jersey. Rather than take the annuity option Greene chose the lump-sum payment of $58,938,743 before taxes. The month following Greene's win the Big Game was changed to the Mega Mil-lions game.

Unlike Erika Greene, who had never bought lottery tickets

before that Tuesday in April, Maurizo Badolato spent one hundred to two hundred dollars per day on lottery tickets. In his case, though, it paid off—he has won three times! His first win was one million dollars, followed by a second win of $10,000 and a final win of $20,000. So after these wins did Maurizo take it easy? No. In fact, Maurizo is now known as the "Meatball Millionaire," because most of his winnings went into starting the family-owned restaurant Ristorante Limoncello in Boston's North End. He has worked hard all of his life, beginning as a waiter in Italy when he was a young man, and now he is working harder than ever while sharing his good fortune with his family. The meatballs? They're his mother's own recipe.

In chapter 2, I gave a short history of the Powerball game, and mentioned that the event that really put the game on the map, so to speak, was the giant $295,700,932 that was won on July 29, 1998, by a group that refers to themselves as the Lucky 13. They were an all-male group of workers at Automotive Tooling Systems, a firm located in a suburb of Columbus, Ohio, called Westerville. The group had been pooling their money to play Ohio lottery games, but occasionally when a big jackpot was on the line they would play other games as well. Apparently the July 29 Powerball game qualified, because each member tossed in $10 and two of them drove one hundred miles to a Speedway gas station in Richmond, Indiana, and purchased 130 Powerball tickets.

At 10:59 P.M. in Des Moines, Iowa, headquarters of MUSL, the Powerball drawing machines in the ITC Studios sprang into action. Five white balls were drawn: 8, 39, 43, 45, and 49. Then came the Powerball, number—you guessed it!—13. The only member of the Lucky 13 group to have spoken about the win was John Jarrell, who happened to be sleeping at the time of the drawing. His wife Sandy watched the drawing and wrote down the winning combination. When she compared it to a photocopied list of the 130 tickets the group had purchased she realized they had a winner. She ran to the bedroom, yelled at John to turn on the light, and showed him the winning combination and the photocopy. "We've got it," he told his wife. Ironically, John almost didn't chip in his $10 because money was tight at the time.

The 13 winners agreed to take a lump-sum payment of $161.5 million split 13 ways. That is about $12.42 million before taxes or about $6.5 to $7 million dollars after. The Speedway store received one hundred thousand dollars for selling the winning ticket.

There have been other groups to win Powerball. For instance, in November of 2000, 14 security officers at Sandia National Laboratories in New Mexico each anted up $10 and bought 140 Powerball tickets. One of their tickets was the winner of the $131 million jackpot. The group, who called themselves New Mexico's First, agreed to take a lump-sum payment, which was worth $70,367,010.58 or about five million dollars per person before taxes.

Since it adopted its previous five-from-49 with one-from-42 format and its current five-from-53 with one-from-42 format, there have been several Powerball jackpot winners. The five largest are as follows:

Jackpot Amount	Date	Won By
$314.9 million	December 25, 2002	Andrew Whittaker Jr. of West Virginia
$295.7 million	July 29, 1998	The Lucky 13
$295 million	August 25, 2001	Split by Delaware couple, Kentucky man, Minnesota woman, Maine couple
$194.46 million	May 20, 1998	Frank & Shirley Capaci, Streamwood, Illinois
$151 million	June 30, 1999	Farrah Slad, Brainerd, Minnesota

One of the most colorful lottery winners is Thomas "Hollywood" Henderson. Henderson, who lives in Austin, Texas, was a linebacker with the Dallas Cowboys and played in their triumphant 1978 Super Bowl. In March of 2000, Henderson bought 20 Lotto Texas tickets in an Austin pharmacy and hit a $28 million jackpot. Choosing to take a lump-sum payment, Henderson ended up with about $10 million after taxes.

Dallas Morning News columnist Frank Luksa interviewed Henderson, who told Luksa that people are constantly after him for money. "I've had people call me who know I don't like 'em. I've even heard from people I thought were dead." Nevertheless he bought homes for his two ex-wives and his daughter Thomesa, and has given away $10,000 each to 50 of his friends and relatives. He told Luksa he would include a note with the $10,000: "Don't ask for any more money."

You can see a picture of Thomas Henderson along with a short write-up about him in the June 10, 2002, issue of *People Magazine*. They document the fact that Henderson is a generous guy who is active in service to the Austin community. That same issue has pictures and stories about several other lottery winners, among them Erika Green, whose picture appears on the cover of the magazine.

There are hundreds of other lottery winners all across this country and I could go on and on describing the good fortune and happiness that has befallen them.[*] But there are some other kinds of tales out there as well.

The Bad (or at Least Not So Good)[**]

You would think that winning $16.2 million would make your life a bowl of cherries. Well, for Buddy Post of Oil City, Pennsylvania, it was just the pits. Buddy, a former cook and carnival worker, won a $16.2 million jackpot in 1988 from the Pennsylvania State Lottery. Shortly thereafter his landlady claimed that she had paid for half of the winning ticket and that Buddy owed her half of the winnings. She sued

---

[*] For stories of earlier lottery winners see the book *Lottery Winners: How They Won and How Winning Changed Their Lives* by H. Roy Kaplan. See note 2 in "References."

[**] Some of the factual information in this section was found in the entertaining book *Luck of the Draw,* by Chris Gudgeon and Barbara Stewart. See note 3 in "References."

him, thereby tying up his winnings until the matter could be settled. The courts eventually awarded her one-third of his winnings.

It gets worse. Post tried starting some businesses, a bar and a used car lot, but both failed. Then in 1991 he got into an argument over business with his stepdaughter's boyfriend. The argument ended when Buddy, trying to scare the boyfriend away, fired a gun into the ceiling. This resulted in an assault charge, and Buddy was tried, convicted, and sentenced to six months in jail. By filing appeals he has managed to stay out of jail but the conviction still hangs over his head.

There's more. Buddy's brother Jeffrey Post had a plan to get his hands on the prize money. How? Nothing to it; he would simply murder Buddy and Buddy's wife and become the heir to their fortune. Fortunately, the police got wind of the scheme before he had a chance to carry out his plot, and he was convicted in 1993.

Because of his bad luck in business, his legal fees, and taxes, Buddy finally declared bankruptcy; he was over five hundred thousand dollars in debt. His most recent attempt to dig himself out of debt was a scheme to auction off his remaining lottery payments. This scheme, however, was being fought by the Pennsylvania State Lottery. The last news I read about Buddy stated that he was living in a mansion with no heat or electricity.

In September of 1984, 65-year-old Mary Ellen Futch of Riverview, Florida, won five million dollars in the Lotto game. She bought a new house and lavished gifts on friends and family but forgot about the IRS. Bad idea! When Uncle

Sam finally came to collect three years after her win, she faced a five-hundred-thousand-dollar bill for back taxes and penalties. Because she had also made some bad investments along the way, this staggering bill forced her to sell her new house and move into a trailer home.

Futch's story gets worse. For unknown reasons, there was animosity between Futch and her daughter-in-law. Futch's solution? Hire a contract killer to murder the woman. Unfortunately for Mary Ellen the person she tried to hire was an undercover cop whom she paid five thousand dollars to do the hit. She was arrested and convicted for conspiracy to commit murder. Whew!

Remember the 1994 romantic comedy *It Could Happen to You*? Nicholas Cage plays a cop who tips a waitress, played by Bridget Fonda, by promising her half of his lottery ticket. When he wins, he splits the prize with Fonda, divorces his greedy wife, and he and Fonda fall in love. Nice story, but it didn't happen that way. The story is based on two real-life people, Bob Cunningham and Phyllis Penzo. Though Cunningham was a police officer and Penzo a waitress, they were (and are) simply friends who split a lottery ticket. Both are married and neither left their spouse for the other.

Now, if the movie producers wanted a true-life story of someone leaving a waitress a lottery ticket as a tip, they would have told the story of Edward Seward Jr. and Tonda Dickerson. It wouldn't have been a romantic comedy though. In 1999, Mr. Seward tipped Dickerson, a waitress at the Gulf Coast Waffle House in Grand Bay, Alabama, with a lottery ticket for the March 6 Florida Lotto drawing. The ticket was a $10 million winner.

It turns out that Seward, who was a regular at the waffle house, had also given tickets to other workers there: Matthew Adams, Sandra Deno, Jackie Fairly, and Angela Tisdale. These folks claimed that there was a standing verbal agreement among the five workers that any winning lottery tickets would be shared equally. This claim was supported by Seward, who said, in addition, that if there were any big winners the five had agreed to buy him a new pickup truck.

Dickerson would have none of it. She, her husband James, and three other family members set up a corporation called Nine Mil shortly after the win and said that there was no such verbal agreement, and the money would go to the corporation. The other four employees filed a lawsuit against Dickerson, claiming she had violated an agreement. They also filed a civil conspiracy complaint against the other Dickerson family members.

The case went to trial on April 19, 1999, and a jury ruled that Mrs. Dickerson would have to share the prize with the other four employees. Dickerson appealed and, in 2000, the state Supreme Court reversed the decision, thereby allowing her to keep all of the prize money. That is the end of the story as far as the four coworkers are concerned but it sure isn't the end of the story.

Before her big win, Tonda Dickerson had been married to a man named Stacy Martin; however, she and Martin divorced before her $10 million windfall. At approximately 6:30 A.M. on Friday, February 8, 2002, Martin forced his way into Dickerson's pickup truck and drove her from Grand Bay across the state line to Jackson, Mississippi. Once there, Tonda pulled out a .22 caliber pistol from her purse, then shot and wounded her abductor. According to a local paper, "Authorities said Martin had recently been released from the Mobile county jail where he was being held on a burglary charge after a December break-in at Dickerson's residence."

Dickerson was not charged but Jackson was expected to be charged with kidnapping. As of this writing I haven't heard if Seward got his pickup truck or not.

Just as in the Tonda Dickerson story, the failure to "get it in writing" has caused other headaches for lottery winners and their colleagues. You'll notice the names Frank and Shirley Capaci in the list of big Powerball winners above, and there's more to their $194 million win than meets the eye.

The story begins in Bill's Pizza Pub in Streamwood, Illinois. On May 20, 1998, the bartenders there, Patty Rooney and John Marnell, collected five-dollar bills from several of the pub's regulars and drove one hour to Pell Lake, Wisconsin, to buy lottery tickets on the big Powerball game. Capaci was part of the money pool —in for five dollars. However, rather than just run a lottery pool, the bartenders put tickets in separate envelopes for each of the five-dollar contributors and distributed them. The ticket in Capaci's envelope was the winner.

Upon learning of his win Capici immediately wrote $10,000 checks to Rooney and Marnell, but pub regulars say that he had promised them, and other patrons, far more. The reports have few details of what people expected of Capici, and this is a reflection of the problem, but people are clearly upset with him. In April of 1999, *Newsweek* reported that many of Capici's former friends would not speak to him, and that he was no longer welcome at the pub. His son Tony summed it up this way: "So much has happened that has made our lives so complex. . . . There are too many allegations and too many negative words."

Pat and Erwin Wales are the August 25, 2001, Maine couple mentioned in the list of Powerball winners. They live in Buxton, Maine, drive a pickup truck with 141,000 miles on it and are just plain folk. Erwin mows grass and works part-time at a Speedway station and a motorcycle shop. Pat worked at the Lincoln Financial Group in Portland but is now on leave. For good reason: she was part of a 19-person lottery pool with coworkers who jointly owned 190 tickets on the August 25 Powerball drawing in New Hampshire. In addition, Pat apparently purchased 20 tickets on her own, separate from the 190 pool tickets. You can see it coming, right? Her coworkers claimed that the winning ticket was one of the 190 pool tickers, and they filed suit. Pat's lawyer, Terrence Garmey, was recently interviewed by Katie Couric on the *Today* show, where he said that the suit had been settled in the Wales's favor by noting the purchase times on the tickets. So, as far as I know, this case is settled.

Sometimes such disputes can arise out of thin air. Remember the story of Erika Green? Recall that there were two other winners in that April 16, 2002, Big Game draw. One of the other winning tickets was purchased at the 1-2-3 Food Mart in Hillside, New Jersey, where Angelito Marquez bought Big Game tickets for his lottery pool at the Newark Extended Care Facility. Marquez came down with the flu on the 17th, and was absent from work for three days. Based on this, and this alone, his coworkers figured that Marquez was withholding the winning ticket from the pool and was intending to defraud them. They retained a lawyer. Did Marquez have the winning ticket? Yeah, he had two of them—each worth one dollar!

Greed almost cost one young Iowa man $5.9 million back in March of 1999. Timothy Schultz and Sarah Elder were both clerks at an Urbandale convenience store. Schultz bought a winning Powerball ticket at the store but had borrowed 50¢ of the one-dollar purchase price from Elder. The transaction was clearly recorded on the store's surveillance system. In addition, Schultz had written "Sarah + Tim's" on the ticket. Here's the problem: Elder was only 20 years old, underage in Iowa. Was the purchase legal and, if so, who owned the ticket?

Schultz claimed that since Elder was underage the entire prize was his. Elder had proof that she had indeed provided half of the purchase price for the ticket. What did the lottery do? Nothing. They refused to pay either of them. Finally, Schultz agreed to pay Elder half of his winnings if she would relinquish all legal claims of ownership. On March 4, 1999, Iowa Attorney General Tom Miller, in a five-paragraph summary of the case, acknowledged the agreement between Schultz and Elder and recommended that the check to Schultz be issued. It was.

All of the disputes in the last five stories could have been avoided by using a little common sense, and I'll have something to say about that in the next chapter. First, though, I want to tell you about a couple of really unsavory characters. Although some of the folks in the stories above, or their friends, might make you wince, they are nothing compared to these two.

The Ugly

I mentioned earlier that I have been a professor at the University of Massachusetts in Amherst for 37 years. A few years ago the university acquired a new president, William F. "Billy" Bulger, the former president of the Massachusetts State Senate. A distinguished man and an accomplished politician, I believe Bulger has endeavored to be a good president for the university. His roots are in Irish South Boston, or "Southie," and he was, and still is, an enormously popular figure there. Of the many people that Bulger mentored through his professional years, one was a bright young man from Southie by the name of John Connolly. Bulger steered Connolly to Boston College and then on to Harvard, where he received a master's degree. Eventually Connolly became an FBI agent working in the Organized Crime Unit in Boston, the outfit charged with breaking up the New England mob.

William Bulger's older brother James "Whitey" Bulger was as different from William as hamburger from filet mignon. Jimmy Bulger's first claim to fame was robbing a bank and getting thrown into Alcatraz. He was released early, reportedly for agreeing to be a subject in LSD experiments. Once out Whitey returned to Southie and joined the Winter Hill gang, a largely Irish outfit that controlled crime in the area.

Connolly, in the meantime, had become a legend in law enforcement because of his effective infiltration and prosecution of the New England mob. In 1975, the paths of Connolly and Whitey Bulger crossed. Connolly had discovered a plan by the mob to have Bulger arrested and he convinced Bulger to become an FBI informant. For the next 15 years Whitey Bulger gave Connolly reliable information about the mob. Oddly enough, during this period, several other members of the Winter Hill gang were arrested and jailed, and Bulger eventually became the gang's leader.

The FBI stopped using Bulger as an informant in 1990, partly because his relationship with Connolly was perceived as being a bit too cozy. In 1991, the Massachusetts State Lottery announced that James Bulger, brother of then–State Senate president William Bulger, and several of James's friends had cashed in a $14 million Mass Millions lottery ticket. By 1994, after deducting taxes, they had been paid installments worth $1.9 million. It was at this time that Bulger disappeared. It turned out that John Connolly, by then retired, had tipped off Bulger that the Massachusetts State Police and the U.S. attorney's office were close to having enough evidence to convict Bulger, his henchman Stevie "the Rifleman" Flemmi, and alleged New England mafia boss Francis "Cadillac Frank" Salemme. Because of this tip Bulger had fled to New York City with his girlfriend Theresa Stanley for an extended stay. For this tip and other ties to Bulger, former agent Connolly would later be charged with racketeering and obstruction of justice. On July 11, 2002, he was found guilty and the story was aired on CBS's *Sixty Minutes* on Sunday, July 14.

On January 5, 1995, Bulger and Ms. Stanley were returning to Boston, reportedly because she was homesick and missed her children. By this time the police and the U.S. attorney had amassed enough evidence to convict Bulger, Flemmi, and Salemme, and on January 5 they succeeded in capturing Flemmi; Salemme was later captured in Florida. Bulger was nowhere to be found. Here's why. As Bulger approached Boston on that January day he heard a radio report about Flemmi's capture. Bulger immediately headed back to New York City and spent the night. The very next day he returned to Boston, dropped off Ms. Stanley in a parking lot, picked up his other girlfriend, Catherine Greig, and vanished into thin air. Although there have been reports of sightings in California, Iowa, and Alabama, both remain at large. Whitey Bulger is on the top of the FBI's Most Wanted list and there is a one-million-dollar reward for information leading to his capture. His traveling companion, Catherine Greig, is wanted for harboring a fugitive.

Whatever happened to that lottery money? It turned out that Bulger hadn't really won the lottery. Rather, he had paid two million dollars in cash for the ticket with the understanding that the future payments would be shared with the ticket's owners. It was nothing but a scheme to launder dirty money. When he and Greig disappeared the U.S. attorney seized the lottery winnings. Bulger's sister, Jean Holland, has been fighting for the past seven years to have herself declared as her brother's legal receiver, but the courts have denied her, ruling that she has not proven Bulger to be absent from the state on a "continuous and long-term basis."

The most recent development involves a rumor that William Bulger had been contacted by Whitey but William had not reported this to the authorities. When asked about this at a recent hearing, William Bulger "took the Fifth." This story is certainly not over yet!

Whitey Bulger's story is ugly, but this next one is worse. On June 28, 1997, a Haitian refugee by the name of Carl Dorelien was the winner of a $3.2 million jackpot in the Florida lottery. The information in the lottery's press releases, no doubt supplied by Dorelien, told a heartwarming story. Carl was so poor that he had to borrow bus fare for the trip to Tallahassee to receive his prize. He told reporters that he was a poor former Haitian army officer who had come to the United States two years earlier to seek political asylum. He said he had been living with his aunt because he had been unable to find work. As it turned out, Carl Dorelien wasn't exactly telling the truth.

Sometimes winning a lottery isn't worth the publicity that it brings. Folks started taking a closer look at Dorelien. It turned out that Dorelien had been a colonel and head of personnel for the Haitian army, an offspring from the group that had seized power from President Jean-Bertrand Aristide in a 1991 coup. Dorelien had been in charge of a seven-thousand-man force. During the period from 1991 to 1994, this group was responsible for hundreds of human rights violations that included kidnapping, murder, rape, and torture. One of the bloodiest was the April 1994 massacre in the Roboteau neighborhood in the northwest city of Gonaïves.

Late in 1994, because of the brutality of the Haitian regime, President Clinton dispatched 20,000 U.S. troops to Haiti to reinstate the deposed Aristide. In a bitter twist of irony, a U.S. military attaché, Lieutenant Colonel Steven Lavasz, part of the team that was then ousting Dorelien and his ilk, issued Dorelien a U.S. visa good for five years and enabled him to "escape" to the United States. Later the Aristide government convicted Dorelien and several others for their roles in the Roboteau massacre and jailed those who remained in Haiti.

In June of 2001 the INS arrested Carl Dorelien. He is currently being held in the Krome Detention Center in Maimi-Dade and is appealing his deportation order. I'll bet he wishes he had never won that $3.2 million in the Florida lottery. I know I wouldn't change places with him.

5

Realities

The Lure

So why do people gamble? The most obvious answer, I suppose, is that they want to get something for nothing. However, I believe, there are deeper and more complex reasons. One reason is entertainment. The Swiss historian Jacob Burckhardt (1818–97) made the following rather incisive observation about the human condition: "Neither in the life of the individual nor in that of mankind is it desirable to know the future." Let me illustrate this with an example of how his philosophy applies to gambling as a form of entertainment. Suppose that I (foolishly) design a slot machine with the following feature: after each spin of the reels a display appears telling the player what the next set of reel stopping positions will be. Though this design is just as big a gamble as a normal slot machine I would be surprised to see anybody playing it.[*]

The reason is that my machine lacks that element crucial to all gambling games—suspense. In the history of gambling, there is no more dramatic illustration of the player's attraction to the element of suspense than in the work of Charles August Fey (1862–1944). Here is his story.

San Francisco before the turn of the century was a rollicking town in which saloons, honky-tonks, and brothels occupied the racier sections of the city, notably the Tenderloin and Barbary Coast sections. Not surprisingly there was gambling present, some of it in the form of gambling machines that were manufactured right in San Francisco by several companies.[4] In 1899, a Bavarian immigrant by the name of Charles August Fey, owner of one of the firms producing such machines, created a gambling device called the Liberty Bell, which all agree is the forerunner of the modern slot machine. It was a huge success. Fey's device was a three-reel, staggered-stop, automatic payout machine, very similar to what you see today but without lights and sound. In my opinion, the primary feature that made Fey's machine a success was not the three reels nor the automatic payout, but the staggered-stop feature. The first reel would stop spinning before the second, which would stop before the third. This added an element of suspense to the game—

---

[*] Around the turn of the century, a variation of this was actually built. Coins won were deposited in a container visible to the player and were released on the next play. The argument was that, since the player knew the result on the next play, it did not constitute gambling. The argument didn't fly.

if the first reel showed a winning symbol, then perhaps the second reel would as well—even though, as today, the suspense was measured in seconds. The original design of Fey's, three reels with a staggered stop, is still the standard for modern gambling machines. Of the many gambling machines manufactured around the turn of the century, the Liberty Bell is the only one that resembles any modern gambling machine. Fey's exploitation of the element of suspense in gambling is phenomenal; more casino floor space is devoted to slot machines than any other gambling game.

All gambling games have this element of suspense, including lotteries. Those Keno balls don't all pop out at once; that roulette ball takes its time dropping into the bowl; and there are sometimes days between the purchase of a lottery ticket and the lottery draw. But the lottery is the worst of all the games. Take a look at figure 17. There I list several gambling games and their corresponding house edges. The numbers assume that for games that involve some degree of skill that the player is playing optimum strategy. Notice that state lottery games have the largest house edges on the list. So why would someone opt to play the lottery instead of some of the other games listed?

Perhaps because the lottery is more convenient; other games require that you travel to a casino or a racetrack. However, that answer doesn't jibe with my observations in Primm, Nevada. There are plenty of good games right in Las Vegas, yet those folks traveled 40 or more miles to buy lottery tickets and stand in 112-degree heat. No, convenience doesn't seem to be the answer.

FIGURE 17

Typical House Edges for Gambling Games

GAME	HOUSE EDGE	GAME	HOUSE EDGE
State Lottery	45% to 55%	Baccarat (Banker)	1.06%
Lottery Keno	30% to 40%	Baccarat (Player)	1.14%
Casino Keno	20% to 30%	Caribbean Stud	5.22%
Scratchers	25% to 45%	Let It Ride	2.865%
Slots	0% to 20%	Three-Card Poker	2.015%
Video Poker	-1.5% to 6%	Blackjack	-2% to 1%
Roulette	5.28%	Horse Racing	15% to 17%
Craps (Pass)	1.41%		

I think that the correct answer is twofold. First, the lottery is, ostensibly, inexpensive compared to the other games listed. I say "ostensibly" because there is the potential for addictive behavior to turn it into an expensive proposition; I'll explore this a bit later. Secondly, and perhaps more significantly, the lottery is selling dreams, the kind of dreams not offered by the other games. When a player buys that lotto ticket, the period of suspense is long enough that they can hold that potential windfall in their hand and dream about all of the things that they are going to do if their lucky day arrives. Buy a new house, buy a sports car, wear two-thousand-dollar suits. Take a cruise, get a facelift, buy rounds of drinks at the local watering hole. Run for office, give money away, be the most popular guy (or gal) in town. They can see it all now. All of these happy thoughts for a lousy buck. Hey, what's not to like?

I mentioned at the end of chapter 2 that two lottery games

changed while I was writing this book. One was the demise of the MUSL game Rolldown and its replacement with a Powerball-type game called Hot Lotto. The other was the replacement of the interstate game the Big Game with a game called Mega Millions. In both instances existing games were replaced by games in which the jackpot is harder to hit than it was in the replaced games; Mega Millions is especially hard to hit, with the chances of doing so being 1 in 135,145,920. Why make such a change? Because such games will produce huge jackpots and these enormous jackpots inspire people's dreams. These are the types of games that lottery players want. They are the only lottery games in which winning the jackpot is not just a financial boost but also a life-altering phenomenon. That is the lure. People are willing to accept a large house edge for a chance at this dream, and that is why they play.

Chances

One of the not-so-nice charges leveled at state lotteries is that they encourage irresponsible behavior, especially in the poor. Indeed, while the state lotteries do publish the player's chances of winning in each of their games (though not the house edge), I feel that they do not put these numbers in proper context. Part of the fault may just be the times in which we live. With politicians tossing around dollar figures of billions and trillions, a 1 in 120,526,770 chance of winning a jackpot might not sound so unreasonable, especially to the largely uneducated poor. Couple this with billboards and TV spots showing happy winners, and it would seem

129

like a few years spent playing the lottery ought to solve one's problems. There was even a woman who tried to sue the Pennsylvania State Lottery because after all of her expenditures on the lottery she'd never won (*Harper's,* September 1994). Let's take a closer look.

Suppose that, in a series of repeated trials of a game, one has a probability p of winning and probability q of losing at each trial. Let's let the symbol E represent the expected number (average number) of trials one can expect until a win occurs. At the very first trial the probability of a win is p and the corresponding number of trials is 1. The probability of a loss is q and the expected number of trials in this case is 1 plus the expected number of remaining trials, which is again E. Weighting 1 and $1 + E$ by their respective probabilities we have

$$E = p \cdot 1 + q(1 + E) \qquad (33)$$

Since $p + q = 1$, we can replace q in (33) by $1 - p$ and solve for E. A bit of simple algebra yields

$$E = \frac{1}{p} \qquad (34)$$

Thus if the probability of winning a single lottery jackpot is 1 in 120,526,770, the average number of games one would have to play before a win occurred would be 120,526,770 of them. If the game were played twice a week this would mean that, on average, one would have to play for 1,158,911 years before seeing a win. Of course you could cut this down by playing $100 each game; then it would only take 11,589 years on average. Sort of puts it into perspective, doesn't it?

Don't think that I'm telling you not to play; I'm just telling you not to expect to win. Let me use the Powerball game to illustrate the point. Out of 120,526,770 players we expect one winner. Referring to figure 7 on page 71, $20,888,592 is distributed among the remaining 120,526,769 players, an average of about 17¢ per player. So, if you play the lottery regularly, expect to lose money.

How Much Money Should I Play?

Good question. I don't know the answer but I have a suggestion. Ask yourself how much money you would be willing to give to charity in your most generous, give-till-it-hurts mode. Take half of that and indeed give it to charity, then gamble with as much of the other half as you wish; if you lose it's still going for a good cause.

Related to this question is the matter of handling your personal finances and compulsive behavior. There is no question that there are compulsive lottery players. Articles can be found on the Internet about people such as the 88-year-old Florida widow who gets four hundred dollars a month from Social Security and yet spends $20 to $30 a week on lottery tickets. Clearly she has a problem. To be fair to the state lotteries, however, a 1996 Minnesota study by Stinchfield and Winters of 944 gamblers in treatment for compulsive gambling found that 37 percent listed slot machines and 37 percent listed card games as their game of choice. Dice games and lottery games were each named by less than 1 percent of those in the study. Nevertheless, pathological lottery play does exist, and if you suspect that you are out of control you should call the National Council on Problem Gambling at 800-522-4700; they will help you.

Here's something else to ponder; I'll use a TV program to illustrate it. PBS carries a program called *Money Moves*, hosted by Jack Gallagher. One of his "Hot Topics" was a program called "Numbers Game" (episode 223). The subject was a 23-year-old California woman by the name of Amber Aase. For the five years prior to filming Ms. Aase had spent $10 to $20 a week on the lottery, sometimes even more when there were large jackpots. Her investment in the lottery during that period was more than $3,100, and she estimated her winnings at three hundred dollars. Financial planner Carol Van Bruggen was asked to comment on Amber's situation. Ms. Van Bruggen played out a scenario in which, rather than playing the lottery, Amber had invested her money and had received a 12 percent rate of return, a bit high by today's standards. Nevertheless, here is what she said: *"Over a five-year period of time, she actually would have had $4,088. But what is amazing is: if she continued to do this, she would have . . . almost $312,000 by the age of 50."*

Even though Ms. Van Bruggen's rate of return was a bit high in my opinion, her point is well taken. Amber admitted that she plays more when she can least afford it, hoping to get money to pay her bills. Bad idea! The best thing you can do for yourself in terms of handling your finances is to pay yourself first by having a regular savings plan. Playing the lottery or any other form of gambling should be the *last* thing on your list, not the first. If you have put away your savings and genuinely have money left over that you don't need for other things, give some of it to charity and gamble with the rest. If you can afford it, and the lottery is your dream, may Lady Luck be with you!

Tips

It should be clear to you by now that I can't give you any winning strategies for playing the lottery. Which brings me to my first tip: *don't let anyone else tell you that they have a winning strategy for playing the lottery either; it's simply rubbish.* There are characters out there that will offer to sell you such strategies. Don't buy them; they are worthless. Most such strategies are based on either a belief that if some numbers haven't appeared for awhile they are "due" or a belief that if some numbers have appeared often the game is biased. Both are crazy. The lottery goes to great lengths to insure that the draw is not biased and that each drawing is independent from the last. Here is MUSL's statement on the randomness and independence of their drawings:

> We work very hard to ensure that the numbers are truly random. Besides making sure that the balls are equal in size, weight, and density, we also randomly rotate between four ball sets (a total of eight sets for the two colors) and two draw machines for each color. We chart the results of the drawings and the pre- and post-draw tests to watch for any behavior that falls outside of statistical expectations. If a ball set does fall outside of our very unreasonable standards for randomness, we pull it and test it with a greater number of ball drops to

ensure it is random. In addition, each ball set is put through very precise measurement by a government lab and is X-rayed at least annually.

MUSL does this explicitly because they don't want to be beaten—and believe me, they aren't. Other lotteries take similar steps.

If you buy lottery tickets keep them in a safe place. If you have a flatbed scanner in your home, make a copy of the ticket and put it in another safe location such as your car. Why? Even if the ticket is in a metal box a fire will destroy it. There have been instances of people losing lottery tickets but because they had proof that they had indeed owned the winning ticket they were awarded the prize. You should also write your name somewhere on the ticket with the words "ticket owner."

Lucky numbers aren't so lucky when it comes to payoffs. Numbers such as 7, 11, and 13 get heavy play, as do numbers such as 19 that are part of birth dates. *What you want is a set of numbers that no one else has.* This way, if you do win, you'll be the only winner and won't have to share the prize. The best way to do this is to wait until the drawing time is near and then buy a quick pick, that is, let the lottery computer pick your numbers. Most, if not all, of these quick-pick schemes are designed to give you a set of numbers that hasn't been played up to that point in time. Any set of numbers is as likely to occur as any other set, so there is no disadvantage to playing this way.

Remember to check your tickets after the drawing. Though this sounds like a no-brainer, there are hundreds of unclaimed lottery tickets each year. Most of these are one-dollar winners but there are bigger figures as well. In March of 1998 a $34 million Lotto jackpot in Michigan went unclaimed. It has been estimated that about 12 percent of lottery tickets go unclaimed (see the FAQs on MUSL's Web site: *www.musl.com*). So don't throw that ticket in the back of your sock drawer and forget that it's there; always check your tickets.

There are some other tips that I want to give you, but I'm going to devote full sections to them to help emphasize them.

Don't Get Scammed

In April of 2002, the San Antonio Police arrested Clodoveo Martinez, based on victim's identification of him, as the perpetrator of a lottery scam. This particular scam, known as the "Latin Lotto Scam," has been operating in Texas and preying upon elderly Hispanics living in the area. Here's how it works. One or two Hispanic men, generally from Central and South America, approach the victim and show him what appears to be a winning Texas lottery ticket. The story is that the men are not U.S. citizens and because of this have to show lottery officials some money, a figure such as five thousand dollars, because they need to prove that they are financially responsible. They offer to share the prize with the victim if he will put up the five thousand dollars that they claim the lottery needs to witness. The scam artists take the victim to his bank, he withdraws the money, and then they take it and run. According to Texas Lottery Commission executive director Linda Cloud, "The Texas Lottery never requires any money in order to have a ticket claimed. And a claim is not denied because a claimant is from another country and may be in the U.S. without proper documentation."

Texas is not unique in this regard, and this type of scam has been run in other parts of the country. So if someone approaches you in a parking lot with a sad story and a winning lottery ticket don't take him to your bank. Take a good look at him (or her) and call the police.

Playing a Positive Game

You should pay particular attention to this section because I'm going to say something that you probably won't expect. In fact, people in certain quarters may think that I'm completely bonkers. Here it is: playing a positive game is not necessarily a good bet. What? From a mathematician? That's heresy! Let me explain.

To begin with, you'll note that I made a big fuss in chapter 3 about calculating break-even points for games with progressive jackpots. In fact, about half of the entries in the appendix are break-even amounts for such games. Before I go any further I should explain one fact about those numbers that I have mentioned but did not emphasize until now: all of my calculations assume that the break-even jackpot is paid out as a lump sum. This means that the true break-even amount in terms of the lottery's announced jackpot has to be larger than the number I calculated. How much larger? That's easy. Take Powerball for example. I give a break-even figure for that game as $99,638,178. Powerball pays an annuity of 30 payments over 29 years. Using formula (29) from chapter 3 we simply divide $99,638,178 by 0.514002335, the jackpot multiplier, and obtain the true break-even jackpot amount: $193,847,715. Okay, so I've taken care of that technicality. It really doesn't matter, though, which is why I didn't bother you with this back in chapter 3.

"Well, wise guy," you're probably thinking, "if it really doesn't matter then why did you even bother to bring up the whole issue of break-even points in the first place?" Fair question. Two reasons. First, many players seem to want this information, so I wanted to both provide what facts could be calculated and show them how to determine these numbers on their own. Second, to give them a good excuse. What do I mean by that? If the jackpot gets large and you're just itching to buy a few tickets, you can smugly tell your girlfriend (boyfriend), wife (husband), or parents (children) that you are playing a positive game and therefore it is a good bet. You can even show them my book's appendix to prove your point. Hey, you're smart, you bet by the numbers; no stupid bets for you. Of course it really isn't a good bet but that's just between you and me.

Okay, why do I keep saying it isn't a good bet? Because in all likelihood you're going to lose your money. "But isn't a positive game supposed to be good for the player?" you're thinking. Under the right circumstances, yes. But expectation is an average figure. It is a theoretical number that approximates what the actual average outcome will be over a large number of trials. It says nothing about a single trial. Suppose you calculate the expected outcome in the rolling of a die. It is simply the sum of the integers 1 through 6 divided by 6; the answer is 3½. Now, I defy anyone to roll a die and obtain 3½ as the outcome. No, 3½ is approximately the number you would calculate if you rolled the die thousands and thousands of times and averaged the results. On a single roll it is a meaningless figure. Here is a story that will put this idea into sharp perspective.

The gambling writer Michael Konik recently wrote a fascinating book of gambling stories called *Telling Lies and Getting Paid*.[5] In it he criticizes some players on Regis Philbin's quiz show *Who Wants to be a Millionaire?* Konick's contention is that contestants frequently don't optimize their expected return; they quit before they should. One of the people who did exactly what Konick complained about is my colleague John Grochowski who, as do I, writes for Frank Scoblete's Web site, *www.scoblete.com*. John writes a twice-weekly column for the *Chicago Sun Times* and has written four excellent books on gambling, all published by Bonus Books. John appeared as a contestant on the show and walked away a $125,000 winner. Several of John's readers asked him about this decision vis-à-vis the Konik book. John's answer appeared on *www.scoblete.com* on April 17, 2002, and was right on the money:

> It's been a year and a half since I was in the "Millionaire" hot seat, and I thought all the curiosity had died months ago. Now I've had a little flurry of interest, with half a dozen e-mails in the last couple of weeks. Hence this "Millionaire"-themed mailbag.
>
> Now then, Konik's look at "Millionaire" odds is

correct as far as it goes, but there are factors he didn't weigh.

The basic calculation goes like this. If you feel you have a 50-50 chance of answering correctly and elect to go for it, half the time you'll drop to $32,000, but half the time you'll win $250,000 and still have the chance to look at the $500,000 and perhaps the $1 million question. That makes your average win at least $141,000, which beats $125,000 just walking away.

If you were in that situation over and over, from here to infinity, then without question the correct play would be to go on. But "Millionaire" doesn't work that way. It's a one shot deal. Each player must decide if the risk of dropping to $32,000 outweighs the potential gains. Are there home improvements to be made, college funds to be set up, dreams to be fulfilled that can be done with $125,000 but not with $32,000? Will the jump from $32,000 to $125,000 make a larger lifestyle difference than the jump from $125,000 to $250,000 would?

Without being more certain of the answer, I think it would have made it foolish for me to risk $93,000.

John, I couldn't have said it better myself, which is why I didn't.

Am I suggesting that one should not play the lottery even if it becomes a positive game? No, what I am suggesting is that whether positive or negative you have to ask yourself this: is the jackpot prize large enough that you're willing to risk, and probably lose, a few bucks for the lifestyle change that winning would bring to you? For example, if I were willing to risk five dollars for the chance to make $30 million on a positive game, I think I would be willing to risk five dollars to win $25 million, even if at $25 million the game were negative. Sure, $30 million is better than $25 million, but in terms of what real effect it would have on my life, it wouldn't matter which one I won.

I can't leave this topic without addressing one other issue. Every now and then someone gets the bright idea of "cornering the market." The idea is to buy up a huge number of lottery tickets, thereby making the chances of winning quite likely. As impossible as it sounds it has been tried. In the late 1970s, Tom and Philomena Drake of McMurray, Pennsylvania, made the national news by announcing that they were going to sink all of their savings, everything but their clothes, furniture, and rent money, into buying scratch tickets. They quit their jobs and spent seven hours a day scratching a particular ticket that had a grand prize of one thousand dollars a week for life. After buying 14,000 tickets they finally stopped playing. They didn't win the big prize, which isn't surprising since there were 35 million tickets in circulation. They were lucky, as when they finally did stop playing they were one thousand dollars ahead. Very lucky!

Assuming that you had enough money to corner the market on a particular type of scratch ticket, and had the means to carry out the plan, you would be absolutely certain to lose money. As you saw back in chapter 3, that's the way the game is designed. The only chance for such a plan to work, in principle, is to corner the market on a progressive game that has turned positive. There are, however, several things wrong with this. To begin with, such games involve really big numbers. If you can afford to corner such a market then you undoubtedly have enough money that winning the lottery isn't a big deal. Ignoring this, though, you could still only buy about 175,000 tickets in a week's time. That is unless you had a team of several thousand covering every lottery machine in the state, which would be not only unrealistic for you but also unacceptable to the state. No, just play your few dollars and hope for the best.

Promotions

Every now and then state lotteries will offer promotions as a part of their advertising budget. You remember my linear algebra student who won $180,000 using a free play—it doesn't get any better than that. Unfortunately, because of some scams involving Massachusetts's lottery promotions, the state doesn't offer these free plays any more. But you can sometimes find them in other states.

When the Hoosier Lottery introduced the now-defunct Max Five game (mentioned back in chapter 2), they mailed a coupon for a free Max Five ticket to their VIP Club members and offered radio and TV viewer giveaways. According to the Hoosier Lottery, nearly five thousand free-ticket coupons were redeemed on the day the game was launched. In addition the lottery offered a buy-one-get-one-free promotion for the game. Since the Max Five game offered a 53 percent return to the player, this promotion returned 106 percent—giving the player a 6 percent edge. Since the infrequently occurring large prizes accounted for about 14 percent of the return this wasn't a great bet, but the two lowest prizes had a probability in excess of 0.18 and returned 80 percent, so the game's drain on the player, unlike the big progressives, wasn't so overwhelming. I would have spent a few fivers on this particular two-for-one promotion.

The trick is to find a two-for-one deal in a game returning over 50 percent to the player (a two-for-one deal will double the return to over 100 percent) and a game in which you also have a chance *to repeatedly play the game;* with repeated play the return becomes more and more meaningful. For example, if one of the twice-daily Pick Three games that returns 60 percent were to offer a month-long two-for-one deal, I would invest some serious bucks playing that promotion. Things like this (rarely) happen, but here is a true story for you.

During the month of November in 1997, the New York State Lottery had a promotion using their Quick Draw game. The following is a direct quote taken from a table card advertising the special promotion:

> Win a double dip on Big Dipper Wednesdays. During our "Big Dipper Wednesday Special" promotion November 5, 12, 19, and 26, prizes for all Winning Quick Draw 4-spot tickets will be doubled."

The promotion did indeed run all four Wednesdays in November of 1997. Recall that back in chapter 3 I calculated the return on the New York Quick Draw game as 59.74 percent. With the Big Dipper Wednesday Special the return was double this—or 119.48 percent. The player enjoyed a whopping 19.48 percent edge. Since Quick Draw drawings are held every five minutes from 10 A.M. to 3 P.M. and 4 P.M. to midnight, one can play 158 games per day. What's more, you can play several sets of numbers per game. If one played this game with 10 sets of numbers for $10 per set for each of the four Wednesdays that the promotion ran, one could have had $63,200 worth of action. At a 19.48 percent return such a player could expect a nice $12,311 profit.

I actually know of a pair of mathematics graduate students in New York state who played the game more aggressively than indicated above and won a very tidy sum. What about yours truly? I didn't find out about this promotion until January of 1998, so my profit was one big goose egg. That is why back in August of 1999 when I wrote about this on *www.scoblete.com* I titled the article "Oh, New York, Bring Back those Big Dippers."

So keep your eyes and ears open. As I said above, the trick is to find a positive game that you can play often enough to let long-term relative frequency kick in.

Group Play

As you saw from some of the stories back in chapter 4, playing in a group can lead to hostilities unless everything is spelled out in advance. Even good friends can become enemies because of such misunderstandings. The pitfalls are easily avoided.

At the very least you should draft a written agreement identifying your group by name, listing the name of each member and what responsibility each member has in terms of contributing to the money pool and contributing to taxes should a win occur. The document should be signed by all of the members, each member should receive a copy, and the original should be stored in a safe place like a safe deposit box or a fireproof home safe. If the group changes in any way a new document should be created.

Whenever a purchase of game tickets is made, the tickets should be copied, each player should receive a copy, and the tickets placed in a large envelope, sealed, and signed by each member. This should be stored in a safe place and need not be opened until, hopefully, winning tickets can be cashed.

Here is another idea that was put forth in an article by Rob Sanford, CFP that appeared in Delta Air Lines' *SKY Magazine*. Form a legal partnership using one of those computerized legal programs that have fill-in-the-blank forms. Have a lawyer look it over to make sure it is properly written. Then obtain a Federal Employer Identification Number (FEIN) for your partnership by filling out IRS form SS-4 and send it to the IRS. If you have one of those computerized tax preparation packages it probably has form SS-4 in it. I use TurboTax and it does indeed have the form. You can also get the form from the IRS. Once you have the FEIN, should you win a big prize you can provide the lottery with that number and then each member will pay his or her share of the taxes as a member of the partnership. Why do this? Well, if one person claims the prize then that person has to collect taxes from all of the other members and when splitting the prize money will face additional gift taxes for amounts over $10,000. The partnership avoids that hassle.

Anonymity

While I was writing this book I received a letter from one of my readers with the following inquiry. Is it possible, having won a large lottery prize, to retain a lawyer and form a trust to receive the prize, and by doing so remain anonymous? I really didn't know. Every lottery that I checked stated that winners of lottery prizes had to be identified. Moreover, for the cases I checked in which the winners had formed a corporation, partnership, or trust, the names of the members of each such organization were explicitly identified.

It seemed to me that the answer to my reader's question was "no." Still, I am not a lawyer, and I did not have time to read the fine print in every lottery's charter regarding the matter. So, I asked the question of a writing colleague on *www.scoblete.com,* Professor I. Nelson Rose. Professor Rose is a professor of law at Whittier Law School in Costa Mesa, California, and is a recognized authority on gambling and the law. Professor Rose noted that his answer to me is not a legal opinion, but he did give me permission to quote him:

> The answer is—there's anonymous and then there's truly anonymous. The state lottery and the IRS want to know the actual names of winners. But the lotteries will help to make sure that nobody knows how to find the winner, if the winner does not want to be found. The lotteries actually

advise winners to become hard to find, because they will otherwise receive so many solicitations. Hiding usually means changing addresses and unlisted phones. But it can involve keeping the winner's name secret.

What If You Win?

If you should be so lucky as to win the big one, don't cash in your ticket right away. Immediately rent a safe deposit box and put the ticket in there. Don't tell a soul that you have won. Change your phone to an unlisted number. If you don't have a security system in your home go out and get a good one. You may also want to get a post office box to direct the hundreds of offers that you are sure to receive. Tear up all, and I mean *all*, of your debit cards. You can keep a couple of credit cards but make sure you have the card numbers, and the phone numbers to cancel the cards, in your records (you really should have that anyway).

Depending upon how comfortable you are with handling the huge sum of money that you are about to receive, you may also want to hire a financial planner. You want to decide this before you see a nickel of your prize. If you do go this route, and you should seriously consider it, you want to hire a certified financial planner, one who doesn't sell anything but advice. If a financial planner sells stocks, bonds, insurance, or any other financial instrument, steer clear. The best way to go about this is to ask friends, relatives, or business associates for references, but don't tell them why you want this information; lots of people hire financial planners just to advise them on their normal finances. To generate a list of financial planners you can look in the yellow pages or you can call the Institute of Certified Financial Planners at 800-282-7526.

After you have done all of the above, cash in your ticket, distribute the money in the investments you or your financial planner have settled on, buy yourself a big pile of traveler's checks, set your security system, take a leave of absence if you're still working, and take a nice long vacation with your spouse or, if single, by yourself. Why? Well, if you want to avoid the throngs of folks with their hands out you will need to vanish into thin air for awhile. For another, your life is about to take a drastic turn. You want to have time to think about what the rest of your life is going to look like. When you finally return, don't promise anybody anything. It's okay to give money to friends or relatives but just do it, don't talk about it. Remember, the money is rightfully yours; nobody has a right to demand it of you. When it comes to gifts, be honest with yourself about how much money you really have and what you will need to live in the lifestyle that you have planned.

Most brokerage accounts will offer you a free debit card. **Don't take it.** Tell them you don't want such a card, and, if they won't accommodate you, threaten to change to another brokerage firm. With credit cards, if you get ripped off, you're only liable for the first $50. A debit card can clean out your account like a vacuum cleaner.

Finally, and this is very important, **pay your taxes!** Even though the IRS will withhold 28 percent from your lottery check or checks, your investments should generate lots of revenue and you're going to have to pay prepaid taxes on this considerable amount of money. Make sure that you do. Oh yeah, one other thing. Make sure you buy that sports car you've always wanted.

Epilogue

What do I really think about state lotteries? I think it is obvious from the facts that I have presented that they are bad bets. That doesn't mean that I think that you shouldn't play lottery games. Lottery games have some positive attributes:

- If you are prudent, they are an inexpensive way to have a little gambling entertainment.
- When you gamble in this way—as opposed to at a casino—you don't have to listen to some sweaty ploppy* criticize your play while blowing smoke in your face.
- If you do get lucky and then use your head, your life will be fantastic.
- If you lose, the money is going for good causes.
- Dreaming the impossible dream is healthy fun.

About that last point, remember the Winner Wonderland ticket I showed you back on page 81? Remember that I said I would scratch it off when I reached the end of this book? I've been dreaming about that ticket. Wouldn't it be fantastic

---

* This is a term coined by Frank Scoblete in his book *Best Blackjack*. It is a catchall term for gamblers who are stupid or distasteful in some way. Great word!

if after writing a book about state lotteries I scratched off that baby and won $250,000? My book would be the talk of the town. I'll bet Katie Couric would want to interview me. What a finish!

Well, here goes . . .

FIGURE 18

Don Catlin Loses Another Five Dollars

References

1. John Scarne. *Scarne's New Complete Guide to Gambling*. New York: Simon & Schuster, 1974.
2. H. Roy Kaplan. *Lottery Winners: How They Won and How Winning Changed Their Lives*. New York: Harper & Row, 1978.
3. Chris Gudgeon and Barbara Stewart. *Luck of the Draw*. Vancouver: Arsenal Pulp Press, 2001
4. Marshall Fey. *Slot Machines: A Pictorial History of the First One Hundred Years*. Reno: Liberty Belle Books, 1994.
5. Michael Konick. *Telling Lies and Getting Paid*. Las Vegas: Huntington Press, 2001

Appendix

This appendix lists each of the games available in the 39 venues in the United States that have government-run lotteries in operation. There is no listing for Tennessee because, although voters approved the lottery in November 2002, as this book goes to press the lottery is not up and running. The games are classified according to the definitions in chapter 2, and numbers are provided indicating break-even figures or house edges, each where applicable. The break-even figures are all calculated for lump-sum payouts. You should read the discussion in chapter 5 concerning the conversion of these figures to advertised jackpots. The reason I didn't do the conversion here is that lotteries sometimes change the period of the annuity or the interest assumption used to calculate the lump-sum payout. If such changes occur you can take them into account and still use the figures provided here to make the conversion to the annuity amount.

I will use the notation x/y to indicate that x numbers are chosen from 1 to y. Thus $5/53 + 1/42$ means that the game is a Pick Five + Pick One game and the number pools are 53 and 42 respectively (like Powerball). I also give the URL for each lottery's Web site and, where possible, the e-mail address of the lottery. I have made no attempt to list all of the different pay tables since these can be obtained from each lottery's Web site. Scratch (and pull-tab) returns cannot be determined by looking at the ticket; one must either have details about the pay tables or the return figure as supplied by the lottery. I contacted every lottery in the United States to request that information and heard from 35 of them; my sincere thanks to those responders. I should note that in some cases, South Carolina for example (who responded), one can go to the Web site, click on a particular game, and get pay tables for that ticket. Some of my information was obtained in this manner.

When calculating break-even points for games in which the non-jackpot payoffs are pari-mutuel, I generally used average figures, either provided by the lottery or estimated by me. Some of these estimates are better than others, depending upon how forthcoming the lottery was with information. For Keno games I indicate the edge for both four-spot and five-spot games, where available; the four-spot edge appears first. Some venues only allow one choice for the number of spots (see Michigan, for example), and these games are indicated where appropriate. For roll-down games I report the house edge as jackpot/no jackpot. The letters *DNA* that appear in some entries stand for "does not apply."

Some lotteries offer free plays as prizes. When calculating house edges in fixed-payout games that offer free plays, I assign the fractional return of the game as the value of the free play. This method is explained in the discussion of the Missouri Show Me Five Paydown game in chapter 3. When calculating break-even figures for games with progressive jackpots that also offer free plays, I assign the value of the free play at 100 percent since, presumably, one would not play the game until it returns 100 percent or better. See chapter 5 for a discussion regarding the wisdom of the positive-game strategy.

In the sometimes murky world of estimating lottery parimutuel schemes or jackpot rollovers, it is easy to make a wrong assumption about how things work and I'm sure that, at times, I made such errors. So, if I get a huffy letter from some lottery telling me I have it all wrong, that's great! I'll be all ears when it comes to getting the correct information from them and maybe they'll even put such detailed information on their Web site.

Arizona

Web Address: *www.arizonalottery.com*
E-mail Address: *feedback@lottery.state.az.us*

GAME	TYPE	BREAK EVEN	HOUSE EDGE
The Pick	6/41 + LB	$3,613,588	Variable
Fantasy Five	5/35	DNA	54.8%
Pick Three	Pick 3 Digits	DNA	50%
Powerball	5/53 + 1/42	$99,638,178	Variable

Scratchers Return: 57–64% (calculated)
No game show

California

Web Address: *www.calottery.com*
E-mail Address: Unavailable

GAME	TYPE	BREAK EVEN	HOUSE EDGE
Super Lotto Plus	5/47 + 1/27	$34,000,000*	Variable
Fantasy Five	5/39	$350,000*	Variable
Daily Derby	Unclassified	DNA	Unknown
Daily Three	Pick 3 Digits	DNA	Est. 50% (pari-mutuel)
Hot Spot	Keno	DNA	Unknown (pari-mutuel)

* These are estimates. Both of these games are paid using an unpublished pari-mutuel schedule and the overall expected return to players is not specified anywhere on their Web site. This makes an exact determination impossible, but using payout histories one can make a good guess.

Scratchers Return: 55–61% for $1–$3 tickets (calculated)
Big Spin game show available

Colorado

Web Address: *www.coloradolottery.com*
E-mail Address: Web site submission form

GAME	TYPE	BREAK EVEN	HOUSE EDGE
Powerball	5/53 + 1/42	$99,638,178	Variable
Cash Five	5/32	DNA	44.7
Classic Lotto	6/42	$4,300,000*	Variable

* As in California, this is an estimate because the payment schedule is pari-mutuel.

Scratchers Return: 65%
No game show

Appendix

Connecticut

Web Address: *www.ctlottery.org*
E-mail Address: *ct-lottery@po.state.ct.us*

GAME	TYPE	BREAK EVEN	HOUSE EDGE
Powerball	5/53 + 1/42	$99,638,178	Variable
Cash Five	5/35 (+ Kicker*)	DNA	41.9% (41.3%)
Classic Lotto	6/44	$5,700,000**	Variable
Play Three & Midday Three	Pick 3 Digits	DNA	50%
Play Four & Midday Four	Pick 4 Digits	DNA	50%

* Optional play for 50¢. Number acts as bonus and must be different from first five picked.
** Estimate based on approximate pari-mutuel schedule.

Scratchers Return: 62.5–71% for $1–$20 tickets, respectively.
Powerball Instant Millionaire game show available

Delaware

Web Address: *www.lottery.state.de.us*
E-mail Address: Web site submission form

GAME	TYPE	BREAK EVEN	HOUSE EDGE
Powerball	5/53 + 1/42	$99,638,178	Variable
Lotto	6/38	$2,478,681	Variable
Play Three	Pick 3 Digits	DNA	50%
Play Four	Pick 4 Digits	DNA	50%

Scratchers Return: 62%
No game show

District of Columbia

Web Address:	*www.lottery.dc.gov*
E-mail Address:	Web site submission form

GAME	TYPE	BREAK EVEN	HOUSE EDGE
Powerball	5/53 + 1/42	$99,638,178	Variable
Quick Cash	6/39	DNA	Unknown*
Hot Five	5/33	DNA	Unknown*
Lucky Numbers	Pick 3 Digits	DNA	Unknown*
DC-4	Pick 4 Digits	DNA	Unknown*

* No pay tables available. Worst lottery site I have seen.

Scratchers Return: 66% average
Powerball Instant Millionaire game show available
Video lottery terminals available

Florida

Web Address:	*www.flalottery.com*
E-mail Address:	*asklott@flalottery.com*

GAME	TYPE	BREAK EVEN	HOUSE EDGE
Lotto	6/53	$20,000,000*	Variable
Mega Money	4/32 + 1/32	$790,000*	Variable
Fantasy Five	5/36 Roll Down	DNA	51%/50%*
Cash Three	Pick 3 Digits	DNA	50%
Play Four	Pick 4 Digits	DNA	50%

* Estimates using averages supplied by Florida Lottery.

Scratchers Return: Current 58.5%; expect increase in '03 to 65%
No game show

Appendix

Georgia

Web Address: *www.galottery.com*
E-mail Address: *glottery@galottery.org*

GAME	TYPE	BREAK EVEN	HOUSE EDGE
Lotto South	6/49	$11,500,000*	Variable
Fantasy Five	5/39	$500,000*	Variable
Mega Millions	5/52 + 1/52	$110,402,647	Variable
Change Game	Digits and Letters	DNA	55%
Cash Three	Pick 3 Digits	DNA	50%
Cash Four	Pick 4 Digits	DNA	50%
Quick Cash	Keno	DNA	41.8%/45.7%

* Estimates based on average pari-mutuel payouts of non-jackpots.

Scratchers Return: 60.7% of sales in fiscal year 2001
No game show

Idaho

Web Address: *www.idaholottery.com*
E-mail Address: *info@idaholottery.com*

GAME	TYPE	BREAK EVEN	HOUSE EDGE
Powerball	5/53 + 1/42	$99,638,178	Variable
Wild Card Two	5/31 + 1/16	$900,008	Variable
Pick Three	Pick 3 Digits	DNA	50%

Scratch/Pull return: 65.79% estimated for fiscal year 2002
No game show

Illinois

Web Address: *www.illinoislottery.com*
E-mail Address: *lottery.info@isl.state.il.us*

GAME	TYPE	BREAK EVEN	HOUSE EDGE
Mega Millions	5/52 + 1/52	$110,402,647	Variable
Lotto	6/52	$16,900,000*	Variable
Little Lotto	5/30	$103,000	Variable
Pick Three	Pick 3 Digits	DNA	50%**
Pick Four	Pick 4 Digits	DNA	50%**

* Based on two plays for $1.
** Doesn't include extra wager available having randomly generated prize structure, since frequency distribution of such is unclear.

Scratchers Return: 63.5%
No game show

Indiana

Web Address: *www.in.gov/hoosierlottery*
E-mail Address: *playersupport@hoosierlottery.com*

GAME	TYPE	BREAK EVEN	HOUSE EDGE
Powerball	5/53 + 1/42	$99,638,178	Variable
Hoosier Lotto	6/48	$9,000,000*	Variable
Lucky Five	5/36	DNA	31.4%
Daily Three	Pick 3 Digits	DNA	50%
Daily Four	Pick 4 Digits	DNA	50%

* Estimate using Hoosier Lottery stated averages.

Scratchers Return: 64%
Hoosier Millionaire game show available

Appendix

Iowa

Web Address: *www.ialottery.com*
E-mail Address: *web.master@ilot.state.ia.us*

GAME	TYPE	BREAK EVEN	HOUSE EDGE
Powerball	5/53 + 1/42	$99,638,178	Variable
Hot Lotto	5/39 + 1/19	$8,395,451	Variable
$100,000 Cash Game	5/35	DNA	51.9%
Free Play Replay	6/30	DNA	46.2%*
Pick 3	Pick 3 Digits	DNA	40%

* Grand prize is $15,000/yr for 15 years—$225,000. Amortized at 5%, this is equivalent to a grand prize of $163,480.

Scratchers Return: 61%
No game show

Kansas

Web Address: *www.kslottery.com*
E-mail Address: *lotteryinfo@kslottery.com*

GAME	TYPE	BREAK EVEN	HOUSE EDGE
Powerball	5/53 + 1/42	$99,638,178	Variable
Super Kansas Cash	5/32 + 1/25	$3,895,940**	Variable
Two by Two*	Pick 4—2 by 2	DNA	51.7%
Keno	Keno	DNA	46.1%/45.3%***
Pick Three	Pick 3 Digits	DNA	50%

* This is the same game as Nebraska Two by Two; see discussion in main text.
** Based on two games for $1.
*** Game has Hot Spot bonus feature for $2 and edges are 45.4%/45.8% on four- and five-spot tickets, respectively.

Scratchers Return: Lottery estimate is 56% and rising.
Powerball Instant Millionaire game show available
Video lottery terminals available

Kentucky

Web Address:	*www.kylottery.com*
E-mail Address:	*custsrvs@kylottery.com*

GAME	TYPE	BREAK EVEN	HOUSE EDGE
Powerball	5/53 + 1/42	$99,638,178	Variable
Lotto South	6/49	$11,500,000*	Variable
Kentucky Cash Ball	4/33 + 1/31	DNA	46.4%
Pick Three	Pick 3 Digits	DNA	40%
Pick Four	Pick 4 Digits	DNA	50%

* Estimate based on average pari-mutuel payouts of non jackpots

Scratchers Return: 62–76% on one dollar to $10 tickets
Powerball Instant Millionaire game show available

Louisiana

Web Address:	*www.louisianalottery.com*
E-mail Address:	Unavailable

GAME	TYPE	BREAK EVEN	HOUSE EDGE
Powerball	5/53 + 1/42	$99,638,178	Variable
Louisiana Lotto	6/49	$2,650,000*	Variable
Cash Quest	Groups of 4/50	DNA	50.4%
Pick Three	Pick 3 Digits	DNA	50%
Pick Four	Pick 4 digits	DNA	50%

* Estimate based on average pari-mutuel payouts on non-jackpots.

Scratchers Return: 60–72% based on calculations from Web data. (Lottery quoted me a 60% figure.)
Powerball Instant Millionaire game show available

Appendix

Maine

Web Address: *www.mainelottery.com*
E-mail Address: *bablo@state.me.us*

GAME	TYPE	BREAK EVEN	HOUSE EDGE
Tri State Megabucks	6/42 + LB	$4,206,786	Variable
Tri State Cash Lotto	4/33 +1/33	DNA	49.9%
Pick Three	Pick 3 Digits	DNA	50%
Pick Four	Pick 4 digits	DNA	50%

Scratchers Return: 62% average
No game show

Maryland

Web Address: *www.mdlottery.com*
E-mail Address: *paffairs@msla.state.md.us*

GAME	TYPE	BREAK EVEN	HOUSE EDGE
Mega Millions	5/52 + 1/52	$110,402,647	Variable
Bonus Match Five	5/39 + LB	DNA	61.7%/42.5%*
Lotto	6/49	$11,138,936**	Variable
Keno	Keno	DNA	41.8%/45.7%
Pick Three	Pick 3 Digits	DNA	50%
Pick Four	Pick 4 Digits	DNA	50%

* First figure is for one game for $1; second is for three games for $2.
** Based on two games for $1.

Scratchers Return: 60–76% for $1–$10 tickets, respectively.
No game show (there is a Cash Encounters TV drawing)

Massachusetts

Web Address: *www.masslottery.com*
E-mail Address: *webmaster@masslottery.com*

GAME	TYPE	BREAK EVEN	HOUSE EDGE
Mega Millions	5/52 + 1/52	$110,402,647	Variable
Megabucks	6/42	$4,070,236	Variable
Mass Millions	6/49 + LB	$11,326,496	Variable
Mass Cash	5/35	DNA	44.2%
Numbers Game	Pick 4 Digits	DNA	40%
Keno	Keno	DNA	30.8%/30.0%

Scratchers Return: 70–72%
No game show

Michigan

Web Address:	*www.michigan.gov/lottery*
E-mail Address:	*milottery@michigan.gov*

GAME	TYPE	BREAK EVEN	HOUSE EDGE
Mega Millions	5/52 + 6/52	$110,402,647	Variable
Winfall	6/49 with Roll Down Variation	Jackpot never exceeds five million	41.1% to 62.6%/-131%*
Michigan Rolldown	5/33 Roll Down	DNA	55.9%/49.6%
Change Play	Digits and Letters	DNA	Unknown
Daily Three	Pick 3 Digits	DNA	50%
Daily Four	Pick 4 Digits	DNA	50%
Keno	Keno	DNA	54.9%**

* Figure after / represents 231% return to players based on Michigan Lottery estimates when jackpot exceeds five million and there is no jackpot winner. This looks high to me. Actual returns for 5, 4, and 3 matches are paid in a pari-mutuel fashion from entire prize pool. Jackpot reverts to $2 million at start of next game.
** Player picks 10 of 80 and lottery picks 22 of 80 (rather than 20).

Scratchers Return: 60% average
No game show

Minnesota

Web Address: *www.lottery.state.mn.us*
E-mail Address: *lottery@winternet.com*

GAME	TYPE	BREAK EVEN	HOUSE EDGE
Powerball	5/53 + 1/42	$99,638,178	Variable
Hot Lotto	5/39 + 1/19	$8,395,451	Variable
Gopher Five	5/44	$618,668	Variable
Daily Three	Pick 3 Digits	DNA	50%

Scratchers Return: 64% (calculated)
Powerball Instant Millionaire game show available

Missouri

Web Address: *www.molottery.state.mo.us*
E-mail Address: *webmail@molottery.com*

GAME	TYPE	BREAK EVEN	HOUSE EDGE
Powerball	5/53 + 1/42	$99,638,178	Variable
Show Me Five Paydown	5/44 Roll Down	DNA	82.6%/52.6%
Lotto	6/44	$5,740,000*	Variable
Keno	Keno	DNA	40.3%/39.7%
Pick Three	Pick 3 digits	DNA	40%
Pick Four	Pick 4 Digits	DNA	40%

* Estimate based on Missouri Lottery published averages. Two plays for $1.

Scratchers Return: 62–68%
Fun & Fortune Wheel Spin available

Montana

Web Address:	*www.montanalottery.com*		
E-mail Address:	*montanalottery@mail.com*		

GAME	TYPE	BREAK EVEN	HOUSE EDGE
Powerball	5/53 + 1/42	$99,638,178	Variable
Hot Lotto	5/39 + 1/19	$8,395,451	Variable
Montana Cash	5/37	$322,297*	Variable
Wild Card Two	5/31 + 1/16	$2,001,516*	Variable

* Based on two plays for $1 or 50¢ per game.

Scratchers Return: 55%
No game show

Nebraska

Web Address:	*www.nelottery.com*		
E-mail Address:	Unavailable		

GAME	TYPE	BREAK EVEN	HOUSE EDGE
Powerball	5/53 + 1/42	$99,638,178	Variable
Pick Five	5/38	$325,612	Variable
Two by Two	2/26 + 2/26	DNA	51.7%

Scratchers Return: 55–65%
No game show (Powerball game show ended April 6, 2002)

New Hampshire

Web Address: *www.nhlottery.org*
E-mail Address: Unavailable

GAME	TYPE	BREAK EVEN	HOUSE EDGE
Powerball	5/53 + 1/42	$99,638,178	Variable
Hot Lotto	5/39 + 1/19	$8,395,451	Variable
Tri State Megabucks	6/42 + LB	$4,206,786	Variable
Tri State Cash Lotto	4/33 + 1/33	DNA	49.9%
Pick Three	Pick 3 Digits	DNA	50%
Pick Four	Pick 4 Digits	DNA	50%

Scratch Return: 64.5% average.
Powerball Instant Millionaire game show available

New Jersey

Web Address: *www.state.nj.us/lottery*
E-mail Address: *publicinfo@lottery.state.nj.us*

GAME	TYPE	BREAK EVEN	HOUSE EDGE
Mega Millions	1/52 + 1/52	$110,402,647	Variable
Jersey Cash Five	5/38 Roll Down	DNA	70.1%*
Pick Six Lotto	6/44	$11,788,236**	Variable
Lotzee	Groups of 4/77	DNA	50.7%
Pick Three***	Pick 3 Digits	DNA	45%
Pick Four***	Pick 4 Digits	DNA	44.2%

* Pari-mutuel game. Calculations based on New Jersey averages. If no jackpot, prize rolls down to second-place winners.
** Pari-mutuel game. Calculations based on New Jersey averages.
*** A bonus match feature is available on these games.

Scratchers Return: 64.37%
No game show

Appendix

New Mexico

Web Address: *www.nmlottery.com*
E-mail Address: *webmaster@nmlottery.com*

GAME	TYPE	BREAK EVEN	HOUSE EDGE
Powerball	5/53 + 1/42	$99,638,178	Variable
Road Runner Cash	5/31	$127,661	Variable
Pick Three	Pick 3 Digits	DNA	50%

Scratchers Return: 63% average
Powerball Instant Millionaire game show available

New York

Web Address: *www.nylottery.org*
E-mail Address: *questions@lottery.state.ny.us*

GAME	TYPE	BREAK EVEN	HOUSE EDGE
Mega Millions	5/32 + 1/52	$110,402,647	Variable
Lotto	6/59	$18,500,000*	Variable
Take Five	5/39	DNA	50%**
Quick Draw	Keno	DNA	40.4%/39.7%
Pick 10	Keno	DNA	50.4%***
Numbers	Pick 3 Digits	DNA	50%
Win Four	Pick 4 Digits	DNA	50%

* This game rolls over both first and second prizes. Hence, this figure represents the sum of first and second place prizes needed for 100% payback. Computations based on N.Y. prize pool percentages.
** Top prize rolls down to second place winners if no jackpot winner.
*** A ten-spot ticket in Quickdraw has a 39.8% house edge.

Scratchers Return: 65% (Lottery is planning three $10 games @ 75%)
No game show

Ohio

Web Address:	*www.ohiolottery.com*
E-mail Address:	Unavailable (Phone: 216-787-3200)

GAME	TYPE	BREAK EVEN	HOUSE EDGE
Super Lotto Plus	6/49 + LB	$11,853,216	Variable
Mega Millions	5/52 + 1/52	$110,402,647	Variable
Buckeye Five	5/37	DNA	45.1%
The Kicker	Side Bet*	DNA	58.5%
Pick Three & Midday Pick Three	Pick 3 Digits	DNA	50%
Pick Four & Midday Pick Four	Pick 4 Digits	DNA	50%

* Side wager on Super Lotto Plus. Player must sequentially match digits in a six-digit sequence with lottery's six-digit sequence. Prizes for two, three, four, five, and six matches in sequence starting with leftmost digit.

Scratchers Return: 63–71% for $1–$10 tickets, respectively.
No game show

Appendix

Oregon

Web Address: *www.oregonlottery.org*
E-mail Address: *lottery.webcenter@state.or.us*

GAME	TYPE	BREAK EVEN	HOUSE EDGE
Powerball	5/53 + 1/42	$99,638,178	Variable
Megabucks	6/48	$10,812,312*	Variable
Win for Life	Groups of 4/77	DNA	31.7%**
Pick Four	Pick 4 Digits	DNA	33.2%***
Sports Action	Unclassified	DNA	Unknown
Keno	Keno	DNA	35.1%/35.1%****

* Based on advertised 76% return to players and two plays/$1. Optional Kicker bet (two plays for $2) requires approximately $18,300,000.
** This game has a grand prize of $1,000/week for life. I used 30 yearly payments of $52,000 over 29 years amortized at 5%—$839,336. This is an approximation if prize is not paid annually.
*** This is for the Easy Combo wager. The other wagers, Exact and Any Order, are all a 40% house edge except for the Four Exact which is 50%.
**** Optional Special Game has similar house edges.

Scratchers Return: 65%
Powerball Instant Millionaire game show available
Video lottery terminals available

Pennsylvania

Web Address: *www.palottery.com*
E-mail Address: *ra-lottery@state.pa.us*

GAME	TYPE	BREAK EVEN	HOUSE EDGE
Powerball	5/53 + 1/42	$99,638,178	Variable
Super Six Lotto	6/69	$104,916,764*	Variable
Cash Five	5/39	$409,081*	Variable
Daily Number	Pick 3 Digits	DNA	50%
Big Four	Pick 4 Digits	DNA	50%

*Pari-mutuel games. Calculated using Pennsylvania's published percentages. Three games for one dollar.

Scratchers Return: 62.8%
No game show

Rhode Island

Web Address: *www.rilot.com*
E-mail Address: Unavailable (Phone: 401-463-6500)

GAME	TYPE	BREAK EVEN	HOUSE EDGE
Powerball	5/53 + 1/42	$99,638,178	Variable
Wild Money	5/35 + LB	$233,032	Variable
Keno Plus	Keno	DNA	35.1%/35%*
Numbers**	Pick 4 Digits	DNA	50%

*Game has an option wherein player can buy a random prize multiplier for a matching wager. Since I have no idea of the frequency distribution for these multipliers, I didn't address this wager.
** Instant Match side bet available

Scratchers Return: Unavailable
No game show
Video lottery terminals available

South Carolina

Web Address: *www.sceducationlottery.com*
E-mail Address: Unavailable

GAME	TYPE	BREAK EVEN	HOUSE EDGE
Powerball	5/53 + 1/42	$99,638,178	Variable
Carolina Five	5/36	DNA	63.2%
Pick Three	Pick 3 Digits	DNA	50%

Scratchers Return: 63%
Powerball Instant Millionaire game show available under the name *Vegas Jackpot*

South Dakota

Web Address: *www.sdlottery.org*
E-mail Address: *lottery@state.sd.us*

GAME	TYPE	BREAK EVEN	HOUSE EDGE
Powerball	5/53 + 1/42	$99,638,178	Variable
Hot Lotto	5/39 + 1/39	$8,395,451	Variable
Wild Card Two	5/31 + 1/16	$1,800,016*	Variable
Dakota Cash	5/35	$255,982	Variable

*Based on two plays for $1.

Scratchers Return: 60.2–69.8% for $1–$10 tickets, respectively
No game show
South Dakota also offers a video lottery consisting of about 8,000 terminals at approximately 1,400 licensed outlets. Games available are Keno, Poker, Blackjack, and Bingo.

Texas

Web Address: *www.txlottery.org*
E-mail Address: *customer.service@lottery.state.tx.us*

GAME	TYPE	BREAK EVEN	HOUSE EDGE
Lotto Texas	6/54	$21,500,000*	Variable
Texas Two Step	4/35 + 1/35	$1,350,000*	Variable
Cash Five	5/34	DNA	50.6%**
Pick Three	Pick 3 Digits	DNA	50%

*Estimates based on past payouts; both games have pari-mutuel payouts in some levels.
**Game is pari-mutuel but jackpot frequency is high. This is my best estimate of the game's edge.

Scratchers Return: 62–65% (calculated)
No game show

Vermont

Web Address: *www.vtlottery.com*
E-mail Address: *admin@vtlottery.com*

GAME	TYPE	BREAK EVEN	HOUSE EDGE
Tri State Megabucks	6/42 + LB	$4,206,786	Variable
Tri State Cash Lotto	4/33 + 1/33	DNA	49.9%
Pick Three	Pick 3 Digits	DNA	50%
Pick Four	Pick 4 Digits	DNA	50%

Scratchers Return: 64% for $1, $2 tickets; 69% for $3, $5 tickets; 75% for $10 and holiday tickets.
No game show

Appendix

Virginia

Web Address: *www.valottery.com*
E-mail Address: *webmaster@valottery.com*

GAME	TYPE	BREAK EVEN	HOUSE EDGE
Mega Millions	5/52 + 1/52	$110,402,647	Variable
Lotto South	6/49	$11,500,000	Variable
Cash Five	5/34	DNA	51.6%
Pick Three	Pick 3 Digits	DNA	50%
Pick Four	Pick 4 Digits	DNA	50%

Scratchers Return: 60.5–69.9% on $1–$10 tickets, respectively
No game show

Washington

Web Address: *www.wa.gov/lot*
E-mail Address: *directors_office@lottery.wa.gov*

GAME	TYPE	BREAK EVEN	HOUSE EDGE
Mega Millions	5/52 + 1/52	$110,402,647	Variable
Lotto Plus	5/43 + 1/23	$8,763,775	Variable
Quinto	5/52	$1,985,610	Variable
Lucky for Life	4/82 Groups of 4	DNA	41.7%*
Keno	Keno	DNA	49.8%
Daily Game 123	Pick 3 Digits	DNA	50%

*Jackpot evaluted @ $839,336 (see Oregon stats).

Scratchers Return: 60–73%
No game show

West Virginia

Web Address: *www.wvlottery.com*
E-mail Address: *mail@wvlottery.com*

GAME	TYPE	BREAK EVEN	HOUSE EDGE
Powerball	5/49 + 1/42	$63,425,984	Variable
Hot Lotto	5/39 + 1/19	$8,395,451	Variable
Cash 25	6/25	DNA	44.4%
Keno	Keno	DNA	41.8%/39.3%*
Pick Three	Pick 3 Digits	DNA	50%
Pick Four	Pick 4 Digits	DNA	50%

*This Keno game has a Bulls Eye option for double the wager (one of the 20 lottery picks is a red "Bulls Eye"). Edge on this game is 49.2%/45.6% for four- and five- spot tickets, respectively.

Scratchers Return: 70% average
Powerball Instant Millionaire game show available
Video lottery terminals available

Wisconsin

Web Address: *www.wilottery.com*
E-mail Address: *info@wilottery.com*

GAME	TYPE	BREAK EVEN	HOUSE EDGE
Powerball	5/49 + 1/42	$63,425,984	Variable
Megabucks	6/49	$11,925,836*	Variable
Super Cash	6/36	DNA	48.3%
City Picks	Unclassified	DNA	48.5%
Pick Three	Pick 3 Digits	DNA	50%
Pick Four	Pick 4 Digits	DNA	50%

*Based on two games for one dollar.

Scratchers Return: 61% average
Super Money game show available

Index

Index

Index

Index

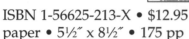